AF890197

SUPREME®
BAR REVIEW

Constitutional Law
Bar Exam Review

Supreme Bar Review
30539 Pinetree Road, Suite 224
Cleveland, Ohio 44124

(866) BAR-PREP (toll-free)

SupremeBarReview.com

Printed in the United States of America.

ISBN-13: 978-1-936450-01-5

For information address:

Supreme Bar Review
30539 Pinetree Road, Suite 224
Cleveland, Ohio 44124

SupremeBarReview.com

TABLE OF CONTENTS

SOME "BIG-PICTURE" ADVICE ON ISSUE-SPOTTING

A. Since the Constitution is a blueprint for the structure of our governmental system, you are probably dealing with a Constitutional Law question if you see any fact pattern involving Congress, the President, or the U.S. Supreme Court.

1. Congress and federal legislative power — Article I and the enforcement powers under the 13th, 14th, and 15th Amendments.

2. The President and federal executive power — Article II.

3. The jurisdiction of the federal courts — Article III.

B. If you see a fact pattern featuring any sort of ***regulatory*** activity by the government, federal or state, you're probably looking at a Constitutional Law question.

C. Since Constitutional Law questions invariably feature the exercise of some governmental POWER, the issue usually falls into one of two categories:

1. SOURCE of power (e.g., Article I, § 8); or

2. RESTRICTION on exercise of that power (e.g., Bill of Rights, which applies to ***state*** governments via the 14th Amendment).

D. Nowadays, questions of FEDERALISM loom large in the realm of Constitutional Law. You are probably dealing with a federalism question if you see a fact pattern with one of the following scenarios:

1. Congress enacts a law allowing private lawsuits against state governments (11th Amendment). (NOTE: Be on the lookout here for any federally-created cause of action that is used by a state employee to sue the state government that employs her.)

2. Congress enacts a law that requires state governments to regulate an activity in a particular way (10th Amendment).

3. Congress enacts a law that requires state or local officials to play a substantial role in administering a federal program (10th Amendment).

Watch Out!

As to these last two items, there will NOT be a federalism problem if states are receiving FEDERAL FUNDS under the program. When states agree to take federal funds, Congress can attach STRINGS to those funds.

4. When Congress regulates purely LOCAL, NON-ECONOMIC CRIMINAL activity (e.g., barring gun possession within 100 yards of a school, as in ***United States v. Lopez***, 514 U.S. 549 (1995)), it may be deemed to have exceeded its authority (Commerce Clause).

5. When a STATE imposes burdensome regulations that inhibit interstate commerce, including protectionist legislation that discriminates against out-of-state products, services, or businesses (the "dormant" Commerce Clause).

Essay Advice

For states that also test Constitutional Law in essay form

Do not be alarmed if a Bar Exam question asks you to analyze a constitutional issue in a lawsuit that was filed under 42 U.S.C. § 1983. Section 1983 is merely the statutory cause of action that Congress has bestowed upon people who are injured by violations of the U.S. Constitution. Section 1983 does not alter, and need not be mentioned in, your constitutional analysis.

CLAUSE-BY-CLAUSE REVIEW OF KEY CONSTITUTIONAL PROVISIONS

CONTRACTS CLAUSE (Article I, § 10)

Source or Restriction:	RESTRICTION
Applies to:	STATES only

Designed to prevent States from passing laws that interfere with ***existing*** contracts (often, but not only, where the State is attempting to evade ***its own*** contractual obligations).

GENERAL WELFARE CLAUSE (i.e., the ***taxing*** and ***spending*** power) (Article I, § 8)

Source or Restriction:	SOURCE
Applies to:	FEDERAL government, specifically Congress

Remember that, when ***exercising*** the spending power, Congress can ***attach strings*** to the receipt of federal funding.

PROPERTY CLAUSE (Article IV, § 3)

Source or Restriction:	SOURCE
Applies to:	FEDERAL government, specifically Congress

This clause vests Congress with broad power to regulate federally-owned property.

POLICE POWER (***not*** in the U.S. Constitution)

Source or Restriction:	SOURCE
Applies to:	STATES only

There is ***no federal*** police power. Only the States have police powers. Congress's legislative authority must be traceable to one of its ***enumerated*** powers — not to any amorphous "police power." State legislation, on the other hand, is routinely based on the police power.

PRIVILEGES AND IMMUNITIES CLAUSE (Article IV, § 2)
PRIVILEGES OR IMMUNITIES CLAUSE (14th Amendment)

Source or Restriction:	Each clause is a RESTRICTION
Applies to:	Each applies to the STATES only

The first clause (requiring intermediate scrutiny) governs state laws that treat residents more favorably than non-residents. The second clause (requiring strict scrutiny) governs ***durational*** residency requirements.

BILL OF ATTAINDER CLAUSE (Article I, § 9)
BILL OF ATTAINDER CLAUSE (Article I, § 10)

Source or Restriction:	Each clause is a RESTRICTION
Applies to:	Article I, § 9 applies to the U.S. CONGRESS Article I, § 10 applies to the STATES

A bill of attainder is a legislative enactment that directs the punishment of a particular person. Essentially, it is trial by legislature — which, by usurping the judicial function, offends the separation of powers.

EX POST FACTO CLAUSE (Article I, § 9)
EX POST FACTO CLAUSE (Article I, § 10)

Source or Restriction:	Each clause is a RESTRICTION
Applies to:	Article I, § 9 applies to the U.S. CONGRESS Article I, § 10 applies to the STATES

An ex post facto law is a legislative enactment that criminally punishes conduct that was lawful when it was done. In short, it is a retroactive criminal punishment.

TENTH AMENDMENT

Source or Restriction:	RESTRICTION
Applies to:	FEDERAL government only

The 10th Amendment invalidates federal legislation that dictates to the States how they must regulate a given problem, or that requires state and local officials to play a substantial role in administering a federal program.

ELEVENTH AMENDMENT

Source or Restriction:	RESTRICTION
Applies to:	FEDERAL legislation only

The 11th Amendment limits the availability of federal causes of action for money damages against state governments.

COMMERCE CLAUSE (Article I, § 8)

The Commerce Clause functions in two very different capacities. It is simultaneously a SOURCE of FEDERAL power and a RESTRICTION upon STATE power.

SOURCE of FEDERAL Power:	The Commerce Clause is an extremely valuable ***source*** of ***federal legislative power***. Note, however, that federalism concerns have prompted the U.S. Supreme Court to limit the sweep of this power.

The clause cannot be used as a basis for federal regulation of purely local, non-economic criminal activity.

But also RESTRICTS STATE Power: The so-called "dormant" Commerce Clause ***restricts*** the ***States*** from enacting laws that burden interstate commerce, including protectionist legislation that discriminates against out-of-state products, services, or businesses.

DUE PROCESS CLAUSE (5th Amendment)
DUE PROCESS CLAUSE (14th Amendment)

Source or Restriction: RESTRICTION
Applies to: 5th Amendment applies to the FEDERAL government
14th Amendment applies to the STATES

EQUAL PROTECTION CLAUSE (14th Amendment)

Source or Restriction: RESTRICTION
Applies to: The STATES

The Equal Protection Clause has no textual counterpart in the Bill of Rights (the first ten amendments to the U.S. Constitution). Nevertheless, it is deemed to apply to the ***federal*** government ***via*** the 5th Amendment Due Process Clause.

THE <u>ENFORCEMENT</u> CLAUSES OF THE 13th, 14th, AND 15th AMENDMENTS

Source or Restriction: SOURCE
Applies to: FEDERAL government, specifically Congress

Known as the "Reconstruction Amendments," the 13th, 14th, and 15th Amendments were adopted shortly after the Civil War. The 13th Amendment abolished slavery; the 14th Amendment imposed significant restrictions (including the Due Process and Equal Protection clauses) on the legislative power of the states; and the 15th Amendment decreed that state and federal voting rights cannot be denied to any citizen "on account of race, color, or previous condition of servitude." Each of these amendments contains an **ENFORCEMENT** clause — § 2 of the 13th Amendment, § 5 of the 14th Amendment, and § 2 of the 15th Amendment — that serves as a grant of federal legislative power to Congress. Each clause vests Congress with the power to ***enforce*** "this article" by "appropriate legislation." The key thing to remember here is that only under the ***13th Amendment*** can Congress regulate purely ***private*** actors. Enforcement power under the 14th and 15th Amendments is limited to the regulation of ***governmental*** actors.

I. POWERS OF GOVERNMENT

A. FEDERAL JUDICIAL POWER

The federal courts are governed by Article III of the Constitution. Article III limits their jurisdiction to that expressly mentioned in Article III and limits federal courts to determining cases or controversies. Article III requires the establishment of the Supreme Court. However, it gives Congress the power to create the lower federal courts and to give them this jurisdiction (or not) statutorily. Finally, Article III protects federal judges by giving them life tenure and salary protection. Federal judges cannot be removed unless they are impeached for high crimes and misdemeanors. Moreover, Congress cannot reduce the salary of a sitting federal judge. These protections are designed to insulate the federal judiciary from political pressures.

The role of the federal courts is to interpret the law, and their control over the other branches of government lies in the power of judicial review. The Court first articulated the power of judicial review in the seminal case of ***Marbury v. Madison***, 5 U.S. 137 (1803). In ***Marbury***, the Court held that it had the power to determine the constitutionality of federal statutes and thus judge the acts of the legislative branch, and that it could determine the constitutionality of the acts of the President, reviewing the executive branch. Although it did not say so expressly in ***Marbury***, the Court later made clear that it is the ultimate arbiter of the Constitution, and that the Court's interpretation of the Constitution has the same force and supremacy as the Constitution itself. ***Cooper v. Aaron***, 358 U.S. 1 (1958). In addition to its review of the other federal branches, the Court may review the final judgments of the highest courts in the states, ***Martin v. Hunter's Lessee***, 14 U.S. 304 (1816), a power which has significant implications for issues of federalism.

1. Organization and Relationship of State and Federal Courts in a Federal System

2. Jurisdiction

a. General

The federal courts are courts of limited jurisdiction and may not hear cases unless specifically authorized by Article III of the Constitution. Article III provides, "The judicial Power shall extend to all Cases, in Law and Equity, arising under this

Constitution, the Laws of the United States, and Treaties made, or which shall be made, under their Authority; to all Cases affecting Ambassadors, other public Ministers and Consuls; to all Cases of admiralty and maritime Jurisdiction; to Controversies to which the United States shall be a Party; to Controversies between two or more States; between a State and Citizens of another State; between Citizens of different States; between Citizens of the same State claiming Lands under Grants of different States, and between a State, or the Citizens thereof, and foreign States, Citizens or Subjects."

In their usual operation, federal courts hear cases falling into two categories. The first category is cases "arising under" federal law, also known as federal question jurisdiction (28 U.S.C. §1331). The second is cases based on state law between citizens of different states, known as "diversity" jurisdiction (28 U.S.C. §1332). It is not enough that Article III authorizes federal courts to exercise jurisdiction — they must also be given that power by Congress. Congress cannot give federal courts more power than that outlined in Article III, but it is not required to give the courts the full extent of the power authorized in the Constitution.

Courts have read the constitutional grant of federal question jurisdiction significantly more broadly than that authorized by Congress in 28 U.S.C. §1331. For example, in ***Osborn v. Bank of United States***, 22 U.S. 738 (1824), the Court held that Article III only requires a "federal ingredient" for federal question jurisdiction. By contrast, in ***Louisville Nashville Railroad Co. v. Mottley***, 211 U.S. 149 (1908), the Court held that §1331 requires more than a "federal ingredient." The federal question must be in plaintiff's complaint to satisfy §1331 — the fact that defendant raises federal law in his defense is insufficient to satisfy the statute.

b. Supreme Court

The Supreme Court has exclusive original jurisdiction over controversies between two or more states, and original (but not exclusive) jurisdiction over controversies affecting ambassadors, public ministers and counsels, and cases in which a state is a party. Original jurisdiction means that these cases can be filed directly before the Supreme Court. However, this is very rarely invoked.

The Supreme Court has appellate jurisdiction over all other cases authorized by Article III. Until 1988, the Court heard some cases on appeal as of right, and others as discretionary appeals by writ of certiorari. Since 1988, however, appellate jurisdiction can only be invoked by writ of certiorari in almost all cases. The only appeals as of right are from orders by three-judge federal district court panels granting or denying injunctive relief. Since such panels are rarely even convened, this exception is quite narrow.

With regard to petitions for certiorari, the Supreme Court has complete discretion on whether or not to grant certiorari and hear those cases. To grant a writ of certiorari, four justices must vote in favor of hearing the case. The denial of a writ of certiorari has absolutely no precedential effect and is not a ruling on the merits of the case.

c. Congressional Power to Define and Limit Federal Jurisdiction

1) General
With the exception of the original jurisdiction of the Supreme Court, federal courts cannot hear cases unless they are authorized to do so by both Article III and by statute. That is, Congress must affirmatively grant jurisdiction. But Article III is a ceiling, not a floor. Congress cannot give federal courts more jurisdiction than is authorized by Article III.

2) Congressional Power to Limit Supreme Court Jurisdiction
Article III specifies the original jurisdiction of the Supreme Court but states that the Court shall have appellate jurisdiction "with such exceptions, and under such regulations, as Congress shall make." Congress can take jurisdiction away from the Court, even in an ongoing case. But Congress cannot prescribe a rule of decision for the Court, and cannot force the Court to rehear a case after rendering a decision. ***United States v. Klein,*** 80 U.S. 128, 146-47 (1872).

3) Congressional Power to Limit Lower Court Jurisdiction
Article III gives Congress the power to "ordain and establish" the lower federal courts and gives Congress discretion not to. Given this discretion, it seems likely that Congress could completely strip the lower courts of jurisdiction over certain subject matters. ***Sheldon v. Sill,*** 49 U.S. 441, 449 (1850).

3. Judicial Review in Operation — "Case or Controversy" Requirement
Article III limits the jurisdiction of federal courts to "cases" or "controversies." In general, this means that courts cannot decide abstract issues of law — there must be a live issue at stake that is actually being contested by interested parties at the time that it is brought before the court. The judicially created doctrines of no advisory opinions, standing, ripeness, and mootness all stem from the "case or controversy" requirement.

a. No Advisory Opinions
Federal courts cannot respond to requests for advice on legal issues. For example, a federal court cannot tell the President whether an action he wants to take would be constitutional. Since the President has not done anything yet, that advice would be based on abstract information and would violate the case and controversy requirement.

In ***Rescue Army v. Municipal Court of Los Angeles***, 331 U.S. 549 (1947), Justice Rutledge explained that the prohibition on advisory opinions stems from separation of powers principles, stating "if government is to function constitutionally, [it is necessary] for each branch of government to keep within its power, especially the courts." The doctrine also protects the interests of litigants, "for premature and relatively abstract decisions, which [advisory opinions] would be most likely to promote, have their part too in rendering rights uncertain and insecure." Finally, he pointed out that the prohibition on advisory opinions is consistent with the Court's unwillingness to adjudicate constitutional issues except when absolutely necessary.

These reasons also give rise to the Court's rulings on standing, ripeness, and mootness.

b. Standing

Except when necessary to redress or prevent actual or imminently threatened injury, courts have no Article III authority to review and revise legislative and executive action. By imposing this requirement, the standing doctrine serves to limit the judicial power in our system of checks and balances. ***Summers v. Earth Island Institute,*** 129 S. Ct. 1142, 1148 (2009).

1) General Rule

In order for a plaintiff to have standing to bring a cause of action, he must have a concrete injury that was caused by the defendant and can be remedied by the court.

2) Constitutional Requirements

There are three constitutional requirements for standing. If the plaintiff does not meet these requirements, then the court lacks the power to hear the case.

a) Actual injury

The plaintiff must suffer an actual, concrete injury. For example, being injured in an automobile accident and requiring medical care is an actual injury. But feeling stigmatized by government support for segregated schools is not a concrete injury and does not satisfy the actual injury requirement. See ***Allen v. Wright***, 468 U.S. 747 (1984).

b) Causation

Plaintiff must be able to show a causal relationship between the injury and defendant's actions. For example, in ***Warth v. Seldin***, 422 U.S. 490 (1973), the Court found that a low-income plaintiff challenging a city's zoning practices on the grounds that they made it impossible to find affordable housing failed to show a causal relationship between the city's practices and his failure to find housing in the city. The Court noted that plaintiff was unable to show that his inability to afford the house was caused by defendant's zoning practices and not simply by market forces.

c) Redressability

The court must be able to provide a remedy for plaintiff's injury. This requirement usually comes up in cases where plaintiffs are seeking large-scale systemic relief and changes in governmental policy. For example, in ***Allen v. Wright,*** 468 U.S. 747 (1984), the Court found that plaintiffs who were seeking a change in IRS policy towards private schools to address the segregation of those schools lacked standing because large-scale changes in IRS policy would go beyond redressing plaintiffs injury.

Watch Out!

When faced with a question based on standing, focus on the requirements for standing and ignore issues of substance in the plaintiff's claim. To determine standing, a court looks solely at whether the plaintiff is legally qualified to press a claim, not whether the claim itself has merit.

3) **Prudential Requirements**
There are also prudential (non-constitutional) requirements for standing. If the prudential requirements are not met, the court may have the constitutional power to hear the case, but there are strong policy reasons not to hear the case, stemming from separation-of-powers principles.

a) **No Third-Party Standing**
A plaintiff may assert only injuries that he or she has suffered and may not raise claims on behalf of third parties. For example, in ***Warth v. Seldin***, 422 U.S. 490 (1973), the Court found that taxpayers who challenged zoning ordinances that excluded low-income housing in their city were really trying to raise claims of third parties, low-income residents, so they lacked standing. There are three exceptions to this doctrine:

i. **Where the third party is unlikely to be able to sue.** For example, a criminal defendant was allowed to sue to prevent race-based peremptory challenges to his jurors in ***Powers v. Ohio,*** 499 U.S. 400 (1991).

ii. **Where there is a close relationship between the plaintiff and the third party.** For example, in ***Singleton v. Wulff,*** 428 U.S. 106 (1976), the Court held that doctors had standing to sue to challenge laws preventing their patients from using contraceptives or getting abortions.

iii. **Challenges based on the overbreadth doctrine.** The Supreme Court "has altered its traditional rules of standing to permit — in the First Amendment area — 'attacks on overly broad statutes with no requirement that the person making the attack demonstrate that his own [speech] could not be [punished if the] statute [were] drawn with the requisite narrow specificity.'" ***Broadrick v. Oklahoma***, 413 U.S. 601, 612 (1973) (quoting ***Dombrowski v. Pfister***, 380 U.S. 479, 486 (1965)). ***Gooding v. Wilson***, 405 U.S. 518 (1972) illustrates how the normal requirements of standing are relaxed in overbreadth challenges. In ***Gooding***, the Supreme Court sustained an overbreadth challenge to a Georgia statute that criminalized a spectrum of statements far broader than unprotected fighting words ("opprobrious words or abusive language tending to cause a breach of the peace," *id.* at 519) — but it did so in a case where the person challenging the statute likely HAD uttered fighting words. ***Gooding*** stemmed from a clash between police and anti-war demonstrators at an army induction center. When police attempted to move the demonstrator away from the facility's entrance, a scuffle ensued in which he said to the officers: "You son of a bitch, I'll choke you to death!" and "White son of a bitch, I'll kill you!" and "You son of a bitch, if you ever put your hands on me again, I'll cut you all to pieces!" 405 U.S. at 520 n.1. Since these words likely fall within the definition of unprotected fighting words, it would have been constitutionally permissible to punish this demonstrator under an appropriately narrow statute. But the Georgia statute was not narrow — and because it swept so far beyond the scope of unprotected fighting words, it was vulnerable to an overbreadth challenge. What ***Gooding*** shows is that STANDING to assert an overbreadth challenge is available even to someone who did *not* engage in constitutionally protected speech and who would *not* have escaped conviction under an appropriately narrow statute.

b) No Generalized Grievances; No Citizenship Standing

A plaintiff lacks standing when she is merely asserting an interest shared by a large class of persons. For example, in ***Lujan v. Defenders of Wildlife***, 504 U.S. 555 (1992), the Court held that plaintiffs who challenged governmental actions having an adverse effect on the environment merely based on their concern for the environment assert a generalized grievance and lack standing.

Lujan was notable because plaintiffs had brought the lawsuit pursuant to a federal statute authorizing lawsuits by any citizens who believed the government was not doing its job. The Court held that Congress lacked the constitutional capacity to authorize such lawsuits because to do so would violate separation-of-powers principles. The Court's opinion in ***Lujan*** appears to say that the prohibition on citizenship standing is a constitutional, rather than a prudential, doctrine, because if it were prudential it could be superseded by Congress.

The Court clarified its position on citizenship standing somewhat in ***Bennett v. Spear***, 520 U.S. 154 (1997), where it held that property owners who challenged a determination by the Interior Secretary limiting the use of their irrigation water because of the presence of endangered species had standing to bring that challenge. Like the plaintiffs in ***Lujan***, the ***Spear*** plaintiffs sued pursuant to a citizenship suit provision of the Endangered Species Act. However, the Court distinguished ***Lujan*** on the grounds that the plaintiffs in ***Spear*** had a concrete interest in the lawsuit that the ***Lujan*** plaintiffs lacked.

As the law currently stands, Congress cannot create a concrete injury by authorizing citizens without one to sue. However, Congress can authorize citizens with actual injuries to sue pursuant to statutory "citizenship suit" measures. This rule appears to conflate the prohibition on citizenship standing with the actual injury requirement and may make the prudential doctrine on citizenship suits obsolete.

c) No Taxpayer Standing

Plaintiffs cannot sue the government solely because they are concerned taxpayers. For example, in ***Frottingham v. Mellon***, 262 U.S. 447 (1923), the Court held that a plaintiff lacked standing to sue the Treasury Secretary to enjoin him from making expenditures pursuant to the Maternity Act of 1921, which provided conditional grants to state programs "to reduce maternal and infant mortality." The Court held that Frottingham's interest as a taxpayer was not sufficient to give her standing because it was the same as that of millions of other taxpayers.

The only exception to this doctrine was created by the Court in ***Flast v. Cohen***, 392 U.S. 83 (1968), where it held that federal taxpayers had standing to challenge congressional expenditures on parochial schools as violating the Establishment Clause. But the Supreme Court has repeatedly stressed that the ***Flast v. Cohen*** exception is extremely narrow. It is not merely confined to Establishment Clause challenges — it is restricted solely to those Establishment Clause challenges that target the **congressional** expenditure of **money** under the **Taxing and Spending Clause** of Article I, § 8. Thus, the Court has held that taxpayers lacked standing under ***Flast*** to challenge the conveyance of government-owned **land** (rather than money) to a Christian college. ***Valley Forge Christian College v. Americans United***, 454 U.S. 464 (1982). And, more recently, the Court held that taxpayers lacked standing under ***Flast*** to challenge discretionary **Executive Branch** (rather than congressional) expenditures that funded religious organizations. ***Hein v. Freedom from Religion Foundation***, 127 S. Ct. 2553 (2007) (rejecting an Establishment Clause challenge to President George W. Bush's "Faith-Based Initiatives").

4) Standing of States as Plaintiffs

In a recent and rare **expansion** of the standing doctrine, the Supreme Court held that **States**, when seeking access to federal court to protect their territorial interests or their quasi-sovereign interests in preserving the resources within their boundaries, are "entitled to special solicitude in our standing analysis." ***Massachusetts v. Environmental Protection Agency***, 127 S. Ct. 1438, 1454-55 (2007). Thus, the Court held that Massachusetts had standing to sue the EPA for refusing to regulate greenhouse gas emissions from automobiles under the Clean Air Act. The Court concluded that the EPA's refusal to regulate greenhouse gas emissions presented a risk of harm to Massachusetts — from the rise in sea levels associated with global warming — that was sufficiently "actual" and "imminent" as to confer standing. *Id.* at 1455.

c. Ripeness

A case is not ripe when there is not yet a live controversy between the parties. It is not enough for a plaintiff to know that someday there may be a controversy; the controversy must be ongoing at the time that the suit is filed.

Ripeness issues usually arise when a plaintiff is suing for declaratory relief. There must be a concrete threat of harm for the cause to be ripe. For example, suppose Ann wants to challenge a state law requiring mandatory AIDS testing of pregnant women. Ann is not pregnant but thinks she might want to be some day. The action is not ripe so Ann cannot sue.

d. Mootness

Mootness is the flip side of ripeness. If the controversy has already been resolved, it is no longer a live controversy and cannot be heard by a court because it is moot. For example, suppose again that Ann wanted to challenge a state law requiring AIDS testing of all pregnant women. Changing the facts, let us suppose that Ann has already become pregnant, already been tested, and already given birth. She can no longer sue to challenge the law — the action is moot.

In some rare cases, the court may recognize an exception to the mootness doctrine for injuries that are **"capable of repetition but evading review."** For example, in ***Roe v. Wade***, 410 U.S. 113 (1973), the Supreme Court heard a challenge to a state law making abortion illegal even though the plaintiff was no longer pregnant at the time the case reached the Supreme Court. Since pregnancy only lasts nine months, plaintiff's injury was "capable of repetition yet evading review" — a case could never be resolved at all levels through the Supreme Court within nine months.

4. Judicial Review in Operation — Political Question Doctrine

General Rule: Some issues are too political to be heard by the courts and should be left to the political branches for determination. This doctrine comes from prudential concerns about separation of powers but the Court has also indicated that it may be constitutionally required.

a. **The four factors:** In the case of ***Baker v. Carr***, 369 U.S. 186 (1962), the Court identified the following four factors for determining a political question:

1) There is a **textually demonstrable commitment** of an issue to the political branches in the Constitution. For example, in ***Nixon v. United States***, 506 U.S. 224 (1993), the Court held that the question of what is an impeachable offense is a political question in part because the Constitution says that the Senate has the "sole" power to try impeachments. OR…

2) There is a **lack of judicially discoverable and manageable standards**. For example, in ***Nixon***, the Court noted the lack of judicially discoverable standards for what an impeachable offense would be in support of its finding of a political question. OR…

3) It is impossible to decide the issue without making **policy determinations** suitable to the political branches, OR…

4) Deciding the issue would create a **danger of lack of respect** for the coordinate branches.

b. The following issues are generally considered to be non-justiciable because they are **political questions**:

1) **"Republican form of government"** — Article IV of the Constitution guarantees that all states shall have a "republican form of government." Since the case of ***Luther v. Borden***, 48 U.S. 1 (1849), Courts have consistently refused to rule on challenges to legislative districting brought pursuant to the Guarantee Clause because they are political questions. **But**, in ***Baker v. Carr***, 369 U.S. 186 (1962), the Court held that it can hear challenges to legislative districts if they are brought pursuant to the Equal Protection Clause of the Fourteenth Amendment instead of the Guarantee Clause.

2) **Standards for impeachment** — The Court will not review the validity of either the substance of impeachable offenses or the process followed by Congress when impeaching. ***Nixon v. United States***, 506 U.S. 224 (1993).

3) **Foreign relations issues** — For example, the question of whether the President may end a treaty was found to be a political question in the case of ***Goldwater v. Carter***, 444 U.S. 996 (1979).

4) **Validity of constitutional amendments.**

5. Judicial Review in Operation - Other Doctrines of Limitation

a. Self-Restraint
As a general principle, courts will avoid deciding constitutional issues whenever the case could turn on a non-constitutional issue. For example, if a case can be decided on statutory grounds, the court will rule solely on the statutory issue and not reach the constitutional issue.

b. Abstention
The abstention doctrines — requiring federal courts to *decline* to exercise jurisdiction over certain matters — apply in three basic scenarios (please memorize them):
i) To avoid interfering with pending state proceedings.
ii) To avoid duplicative litigation; i.e., simultaneous, essentially identical lawsuits in state and federal court.
iii) To allow state courts to clarify unclear state law.

The first category — abstention to avoid interfering with pending state proceedings — is called ***Younger*** abstention.

The second category — abstention to avoid duplicative litigation — is called ***Colorado River*** abstention.

The third category — abstention to allow state courts to clarify unclear state law — arises in three distinct scenarios:

i) Abstention because a state court's clarification of state law might avoid a federal court ruling on constitutional grounds. This is called ***Pullman*** abstention.

ii) Abstention in diversity cases because of unclear state law. This is called ***Thibodaux*** abstention.

iii) Abstention because of complex state administrative procedures. This is called ***Burford*** abstention.

Each of these doctrines is detailed in the paragraphs that follow.

1) Abstention because of unclear state law

When a federal court believes that a case may turn on an issue of state law, and the state law is unclear, the court must abstain from deciding the issue of state law and remand the case to a state court for clarification of that issue. The reason for this type of abstention is that state courts, not federal courts, are the proper forum for determining state law issues. This type of abstention falls into three categories, named after the cases in which the Supreme Court established the doctrines:

a) ***Pullman* abstention** — Abstention to avoid federal court constitutional rulings: Abstention is required when a state court's clarification of unclear state law might make a federal court's constitutional ruling unnecessary. ***Railroad Commission of Texas v. Pullman Co.,*** 312 U.S. 496 (1941). In order for *Pullman* abstention to be warranted, there must be **substantial uncertainty** as to the meaning of the **state law**, and there must be a **reasonable possibility** that determining the state law issue would make the constitutional ruling unnecessary. These requirements are to be read narrowly.

Example: Plaintiff sues a state governmental agency, alleging that its hiring practices violate both the Equal Protection Clause of the Fourteenth Amendment and state anti-discrimination laws. If there is substantial uncertainty about the state courts' interpretation of the state anti-discrimination law, and there is a reasonable possibility that plaintiff could prevail pursuant to the state law claim, the federal court must abstain to allow a state court to clarify the law.

b) ***Thibodaux* abstention** — Abstention because of unclear state law in diversity cases: Federal courts decide issues of state law when their jurisdiction is based on diversity. The **general rule** is that federal courts should **not** abstain from diversity cases when state law is unclear. There is a **rare and narrowly construed exception** to this general rule — when the state law is unclear and the diversity case involves an **important state interest** that is **intimately involved** with a state's **sovereign prerogative**, the federal court must abstain. ***Louisiana Power and Light Co. v. City of Thibodaux,*** 360 U.S. 25 (1959).

Example: In ***Thibodaux***, plaintiff challenged the state's use of eminent domain to take his property where the state's authority to do so under state law was unclear. The Court held that the district court should have abstained to allow the state court to determine whether state law authorized the state to take the property.

c) ***Burford* abstention** — Abstention to Defer to Complex State Administrative Proceedings: A federal court must abstain when it is asked to decide a case that involves issues that are generally determined pursuant to a complex state administrative procedure. ***Burford v. Sun Oil Co.,*** 319 U.S. 315 (1943). Under this doctrine, the federal court must **dismiss** the case, not remand it as in ***Pullman*** and ***Thibodaux*** abstention. ***Burford*** abstention is only warranted when the primary purpose of the state administrative proceeding is to achieve uniformity and there is a danger that judicial review would disrupt that uniformity. ***Burford*** abstention is limited to requests for declaratory and equitable relief, and does not apply in suits for monetary damages.

Example: Plaintiff has applied for a license to sell electrical power in a state where there is a complex administrative procedure for granting licenses, and is denied that license. If plaintiff sues in federal court to challenge the denial of that license, the federal court must abstain if the primary purpose of the state administrative proceeding is to achieve uniformity and there is a danger that judicial review would disrupt that uniformity.

2) Younger Abstention — Abstention because of Ongoing State Court Proceedings: Federal courts may not enjoin any pending state court criminal proceedings. ***Younger v. Harris,*** 401 U.S. 37 (1971). They are also prohibited from enjoining state civil proceedings when the state government is a party, and civil actions between private parties when there is an important state interest involved. Finally, a federal court must abstain from adjudicating matters that are pending before state administrative agencies when important state interests are at stake.

For example, in ***Trainor v. Hernandez,*** 431 U.S. 434 (1977), the state brings a civil action to recover welfare benefits from Hernandez and his wife, accusing her of welfare fraud and simultaneously attaching Hernandez's assets. Hernandez filed a lawsuit in federal courts alleging that the state procedures violated his due process rights. The Court held that ***Younger*** abstention was warranted and ordered the trial court to dismiss the case.

Exceptions: There are several exceptions to the ***Younger*** abstention doctrine. First, federal courts may enjoin bad faith prosecutions in state court. Federal injunctions of state actions are appropriate if the state statute is patently unconstitutional or if there is no adequate state forum available. Finally, the issue of ***Younger*** abstention can be waived, so it must be raised by the parties.

3) **Colorado River Abstention** — Abstention to Avoid Duplicative Litigation: Sometimes when identical suits are filed in both state and federal court, the federal court must abstain to avoid duplicative litigation. ***Colorado River Water Conservation District v. United States,*** 424 U.S. 800 (1976). For example, suppose Ann sues Bob in state court alleging breach of contract. The next day, Bob sues Ann in federal court in diversity, also alleging breach of contract. The two suits could proceed simultaneously; but whichever court rules first will preclude judgment in the other action because of the doctrine of res judicata. Or, the federal court could abstain and avoid duplicative litigation.

General rule: The general rule is that the federal court need not abstain, with one major traditional exception. That exception is that in actions concerning real property, whichever court has jurisdiction first is entitled to exclusive jurisdiction over that property.

Exception — *Colorado River* abstention: In ***Colorado River***, the Court stated that in some exceptional circumstances, a federal court must abstain to avoid duplicative litigation out of deference to pending state proceedings. The Court listed the following factors which must be considered: 1) the problems that occur when a state and federal court assume jurisdiction over the same res; 2) the relative inconvenience of the federal forum; 3) the need to avoid piecemeal litigation and 4) the order in which the state and federal proceedings were filed. These factors are narrowly applied and the federal court generally will only abstain in cases involving the determination of finite resources with a careful balancing of the considerations involved.

In ***Colorado River***, the United States filed suit in federal court, naming 1000 defendants as parties, to determine their water rights. One of the parties filed a motion in a concurrent suit in state court to make the federal government a party to that state suit. Because the four factors weigh in favor of abstaining, the Court held that abstention was warranted and ordered the trial court to dismiss the federal suit.

c. Speech or Debate Clause

The Speech or Debate Clause (Article I, § 6) provides that "for any Speech or Debate in either House, [members of Congress] shall not be questioned in any other Place." In ***Kilburn v. Thompson***, 103 U.S. 168 (1881), the Court first interpreted the clause and found that the clause extends to all "things generally done in a session of

[Congress] by one of its members in relation to the business before it." The Clause insulates members of Congress from liability for anything related to their "legislative activities," including voting, preparing committee reports, and conducting committee hearings. However, the clause does not insulate members of Congress from liability for "political matters" including providing constituent services, aiding individuals seeking government contracts, and arranging appointments with government agencies. ***United States v. Brewster***, 408 U.S. 501 (1972).

6. Supreme Court Review of State Court Decisions

General Rule: ***In Martin v. Hunter's Lessee***, 14 U.S. 304 (1816), the Supreme Court first established its power to review final judgments of state supreme courts. Since 1988, state court decisions can only be heard by writ of certiorari. The decision of whether or not to grant a writ of certiorari and hear the case is completely up to the Court's discretion.

The ***Martin*** Court identified maintaining the uniformity and supremacy of federal law as its reason for reviewing state courts decisions. Therefore, this review is limited to issues of federal law, and the Court may not consider state court decisions that turn on issues of state law. In order to avoid decisions based on state law, and to avoid advisory opinions on federal law issues, the Court has established the doctrine that it will not hear state court cases when they rest on an adequate and independent state ground.

a. Adequate and Independent State Ground

If the decision of the state supreme court rests on a combination of state and federal law, and the state law determination provides an adequate and independent ground for the state court ruling, then the U.S. Supreme Court cannot review the state court decision. The state law ground must be both adequate and independent.

Example: If a state court strikes down a state law because it violates both the state and the federal constitution, then the Supreme Court must deny review because the state ground is adequate and independent. If the statute violates the state constitution, it must be struck down and the determination of federal law does not matter. On the other hand, if the state court upholds the statute against challenges under both the state and federal constitution, the Supreme Court may review the decision, because reversal of the state court's federal law decision would determine the outcome of the case.

1) Adequacy of the State Ground

General Rule: A state court's ruling on state law is deemed adequate if the Supreme Court's reversal of the federal law ruling would not alter the outcome of the case.

That is, the Supreme Court may not review a case where it must uphold the state court decision regardless of its ruling on the federal law issue.

Exceptions: There are several situations where the state law issue is not adequate even if it is the true basis for the state court's decision.

a) **Unconstitutional state law** — A state law that violates the federal constitution cannot be an adequate ground for a state court decision. For example, a state law that prohibits African American people from purchasing real property within the state would not provide an adequate state ground because that law itself violates the Equal Protection Clause of the Fourteenth Amendment.

b) **No support for the decision on the record** — A state law cannot be an adequate ground for a state court decision when there is no fair and substantial basis in the record for the state court's determination of the state law issue. If there is no factual evidence on the record to support that decision, the state law ground is not adequate.

c) **State procedural ground as a subterfuge** — Generally, state procedural grounds are adequate. For example, if a state court refused to hear an appeal on state law issues because the appellant did not file his appeal within the 90 days required by state law, the state court's dismissal of the case is based on an adequate state ground. However, if the state procedural rule is trivial, or discretionary, or if it is manufactured by the state court to preclude review of the federal issue, then the state ground is not adequate. For example, in ***NAACP v. Alabama ex rel. Patterson***, 357 U.S. 449 (1958), the state of Alabama sued the NAACP to halt its operations within the state. The NAACP argued that the state's attempt to close it down violated its First Amendment rights to free speech and assembly. The NAACP lost at the trial level and appealed to the state supreme court, but the state supreme court dismissed the appeal based solely on the appeal brief's non-compliance with technical rules such as the number of pages and size of the margin. The Court held that those technical state rules were a subterfuge and could not provide an adequate state ground that would preclude Supreme Court review.

2) Independence of the State Ground

Sometimes a state court decision is based on a combination of state and federal law. For example, some state laws incorporate federal standards. And plaintiffs often bring constitutional challenges based on both state and federal constitutions. A state ground is deemed independent only if it is based solely on state law and is not tied to federal law.

The rule for determining whether a state ground is independent is simple — the state ground is independent if the state supreme court says that it is independent. ***Michigan v. Long***, 463 U.S. 1032 (1983). The state opinion should assert clearly that it is based solely on state law. If not, the Supreme Court will assume that the state ground is not independent and that it may decide the case. For example, in ***Michigan v. Long***, a state criminal defendant being prosecuted for possession of drugs challenged the search that uncovered the drugs as violating both the federal Fourth Amendment and its counterpart in the state constitution — and the state Supreme Court ruled in his favor and suppressed the evidence. Because the state court opinion did not assert clearly that it was based solely on the state constitution, the Supreme Court held that it could review the case because there was no independent state ground.

B. FEDERAL LEGISLATIVE POWER

1. Implied Powers — The Necessary and Proper Clause

General rule: Congress, like all branches of the federal government, has limited powers. It may only legislate if authorized to do so by the Constitution. If the power to legislate in a certain area is not expressly granted in the Constitution, Congress lacks the power to legislate in that area. However, Congress may legislate when that legislation is "necessary and proper" to carrying out the powers expressly granted to it in the Constitution. In ***McCulloch v. Maryland***, 17 U.S. 316 (1819), the Court interpreted the Necessary and Proper Clause to give Congress implied powers to carry out its enumerated powers. The Court stated that as long as the end is constitutional (within Congress's enumerated powers), any appropriate means for carrying out this end is also constitutional.

The ***McCulloch*** test is extremely deferential to Congress and the powers of the federal government in general. Over the years, the Court has at times taken a less deferential approach to reviewing Congress's power to enact legislation. For example, in recent years, the Court has restricted its view of implied powers, especially in the areas of Commerce Clause legislation and legislation enforcing the Fourteenth Amendment.

2. The Interstate Commerce Clause

The Interstate Commerce Clause (Article I, § 8, clause 3) grants to Congress the power "to regulate Commerce . . . among the several States." Congress often relies upon its Commerce Clause powers to enact legislation. For more than 60 years following the New Deal, the Court maintained an extremely broad interpretation of Congress's legislative authority under the Commerce Clause. But starting in 1995, the Court has restricted its reading of the Commerce Clause powers.

a. When Congress May Legislate Pursuant to the Commerce Clause

1) Use of Interstate Commerce

Congress may legislate to regulate the use of interstate commerce. For example, when Congress enacts laws governing interstate banks or the securities industry, it is regulating interstate commerce.

2) Instrumentalities of Interstate Commerce

Congress may legislate to regulate the instrumentalities of interstate commerce. For example, Congress can regulate railroads and interstate highways because they are used in interstate commerce.

Pursuant to its ability to regulate the instrumentalities of interstate commerce, Congress can prohibit activity from occurring in interstate commerce even if that prohibition affects intrastate activity. For example, in ***Champion v. Ames***, 188 U.S. 321 (1903), the Court upheld Congress's power to prohibit interstate importing, mailing, or transporting of lottery tickets. Congress has often used this "jurisdictional hook" to enact legislation, including the Fair Labor Standards Act and other legislation governing the rights of workers. The Court upheld the application of the FLSA, which prohibited the shipment in interstate commerce of goods manufactured by employees whose wages are less than minimum wage, to local industry in ***United States v. Darby***, 312 U.S. 100 (1941), based in part on the fact that the FLSA was a valid piece of "commerce prohibiting" legislation.

3) Stream of Commerce

Congress may regulate intrastate activity that falls within the stream of commerce. For example, in ***Stafford v. Wallace***, 258 U.S. 495 (1922), the Court upheld the constitutionality of the Packers and Stockyards Act of 1921, which prohibited "unfair, discriminatory or deceptive practices" by meat packers in interstate commerce. The Court noted that the local stockyards were "but a throat through which the current [of interstate commerce] flows," and could therefore be regulated by Congress pursuant to its Commerce Clause powers.

4) Substantially Affects Interstate Commerce

Congress may regulate activity that substantially affects interstate commerce even if that activity is solely intrastate activity, as long as the activity is economic in nature. For example, in ***United States v. Darby***, 312 U.S. 100 (1941), the Court held that Congress may regulate the wages paid by a local business to its workers because the wages paid by the local employer have a substantial effect on interstate commerce.

Even if the activities of the party being regulated themselves do not have a substantial effect, the Court has held that it may consider whether the aggregate effect on interstate commerce of many people engaging in the same activity would be substantial in upholding the constitutionality of legislation regulating that activity. For example, in ***Wickard v. Filburn***, 317 U.S. 111 (1942), the Court upheld the imposition of a marketing penalty on a farmer who grew wheat in excess of limits imposed by Congress, even though the farmer claimed that the excess wheat was grown solely for his personal consumption. The Court said that it was appropriate for Congress to consider the aggregate effect that many farmers growing their own wheat would have on interstate commerce by depressing demand in the market.

During the 1960s, Congress used its Commerce Clause authority to enact civil rights legislation that prohibited race discrimination by private businesses, finding that race discrimination in the aggregate had a substantial effect on interstate commerce. The Court upheld the constitutionality of that legislation in ***Heart of Atlanta Motel v. United States***, 379 U.S. 241 (1964).

5) Federalism Constraints
From the New Deal until 1995, the Court applied the "substantially affecting commerce" test so broadly that virtually any local activity was seen to affect commerce and thus be subject to Congressional regulation. But starting in 1995, spurred by federalism concerns, the Court has insisted that the regulated activity must itself be economic activity — it is not enough that the activity has an economic effect. For example, in ***United States v. Lopez,*** 514 U.S. 549 (1995), the Court held that Congress lacked the power under the Commerce Clause to make it a federal crime to possess a handgun in a school zone. The Court stated that because owning a gun is not an economic activity, Congress could not regulate it under the Commerce Clause. Similarly, in ***United States v. Morrison***, 529 U.S. 598 (2000), the Court held that Congress lacked the power under the Commerce Clause to enact a federal civil rights remedy for victims of domestic violence because domestic violence is not economic activity.

3. The Spending Power
Congress has the power (Article I, § 8, clause 1) to spend money to provide for the "general Welfare of the United States." Pursuant to this power, Congress may attach conditions to the expenditures of public money. Congress's ability to set public policy through use of its spending powers is broad. It will be upheld if the following conditions are met:

a. The exercise of the spending power must be in pursuit of the "general Welfare."

b. Conditions attached to the spending must be related to the federal interest in the funded program.

c. The state's receipt of the money should be voluntary. Congress cannot coerce the state into taking the money and accepting the conditions.

Example: Congress conditioned a state's receipt of federal highway funds on the state's adoption of a 21-year-old minimum drinking age. This was in pursuit of the general welfare because its goal was to reduce drunk driving. Reducing drunk driving was related to building highways because people drive on highways. And, the state could choose to refuse federal highway funds. Therefore this was a constitutional use of Congress's spending powers.

4. The Taxing Power
Along with its power to spend money, Congress has the power to impose taxes (Article I, § 8, clause 1). Congress may use its taxing power to set public policy, as long as the primary purpose of the tax is to raise revenue rather than to regulate. This includes the power to impose personal income taxes and create rules allowing exemptions and deductions for certain activities. **It also includes the power to tax undesirable activity such as the sale of tobacco.** Any tax set by Congress must be uniformly applied

throughout the United States.

Example: Federal laws allowing a taxpayer to take a tax deduction for a dependent child further the policy of encouraging people to have children. These laws are a constitutional use of Congress's taxing power.

Watch Out!

When you see a question on the bar exam that refers to the General Welfare Clause of the Constitution, do not be fooled by its name. The General Welfare Clause of the Constitution does ***not*** give Congress the power to enact any legislation that promotes the general welfare of the nation. Instead, the General Welfare Clause ***only*** gives Congress the ***power to tax and spend for the general welfare***. Thus any reference to the General Welfare Clause is actually a reference to the **taxing** and **spending** powers of Congress.

5. Other Powers

a. Power over Federal Property

Congress has the power (Article IV, § 3) to make rules and regulations governing property owned by the United States, and it has broad discretion to do so. If the federal government acquires land without a state's consent, state law governs that land except to the extent that Congress adopts legislation preempting that state law.

b. War Powers

Congress has the power (Article I, § 8) to declare war, and to raise and support the armed forces. In addition, Congress has broad powers to legislate domestically during times of war. For example, in ***Woods v. Cloyd W. Miller Co.,*** 333 U.S. 138 (1948), the Court upheld a federal law imposing rent control that Congress enacted pursuant to its war powers, because of the country's focus on the war industry rather than building housing during World War II and the demand on housing caused by the returning soldiers. The Court stated that "it is plain from the legislative history that Congress was invoking its war power to cope with a current condition of which the war was a direct and immediate cause." The Court's ruling in ***Woods*** is typical of the deferential attitude that the Court takes towards Congress's use of its war powers, tending to uphold such Congressional actions.

c. Other Foreign Powers

Congress has similarly broad power to pass laws that are necessary and proper to enforce treaties entered into by the United States. For example, Congress passed a law prohibiting the hunting of migratory birds pursuant to a treaty between the United States and Canada that protected migratory birds. That law was found to be constitutional in the case of ***Missouri v. Holland***, 252 U.S. 416 (1920) because it furthered the goals of the treaty — protecting the birds. The only limit on Congress's ability to legislate pursuant to treaties is that it may not violate other provisions of the Constitution (such as Due Process) with such legislation. For example, in ***Reid v. Covert***, 354 U.S. 1 (1957), the Court held that Congress could not provide for military jurisdiction over civilian dependents of military personnel overseas, even though the law was enacted to further the goals of a treaty, because such a law would violate the due process rights of the civilian dependents.

Finally, Congress has complete, sweeping control over determining citizenship and regulating naturalization of new citizens.

6. Delegation of Legislative Power

Congress has wide latitude to delegate legislative power, including policy-making authority, to executive branch administrative agencies. The Court has held that such delegation is constitutional so long as Congress "lay[s] down by legislative act an intelligible principle to which the person or body authorized to [act] is directed to conform." ***Touhy v. United States***, 500 U.S. 160 (1991). The standard is so broad and deferential to Congress that the Court has not struck down the Congressional delegation of power to the executive branch since 1935.

In addition, the Court upheld the constitutionality of Congressional delegation of legislative power to the judicial branch, pursuant to the Sentencing Reform Act of 1984, in ***Mistretta v. United States***, 488 U.S. 361 (1989). The Act created a sentencing guideline commission and provided that several members of the commission would be federal judges. The Court held that this arrangement did not violate principles of separation of powers because there was no danger of aggrandizement by any branch.

Once Congress delegates legislative power, however, it is limited as to how much control it can maintain over that power. For a long time, Congress accompanied the delegation of power with "legislative veto" measures, allowing Congress to overturn executive policy decisions by measures short of enacting laws to overturn them. The Court considered the constitutionality of one such legislative veto in the case of ***INS v. Chadha***, 462 U.S. 919 (1983), and found it to be lacking. In the Immigration and Nationality Act, Congress had delegated to the Attorney General of the United States the authority to suspend deportations of deportable aliens. However, the Act allowed Congress to overturn any individual decision of the Attorney General by majority vote of one house. In ***Chadha***, the Court held this arrangement to be unconstitutional because it did not meet the constitutional requirements of bicameralism (passage by majority of **both** houses of Congress) and presentment to the President.

The Court's ruling in **Chadha** tells us that any time Congress takes legislative action, that action must meet the requirements of bicameralism and presentment. Moreover, any time Congress delegates legislative authority to an executive official, Congress cannot exercise any control over that official. ***Bowsher v. Synar***, 478 U.S. 714 (1986). These rulings significantly limit Congress's ability to attach strings to power that it delegates to the executive branch.

C. FEDERAL EXECUTIVE POWER

1. Domestic Affairs Power

The President is the Chief Executive, and his role in domestic affairs is to execute the laws that are made by Congress. To do this, he is in charge of a large administrative apparatus that carries out the day-to-day operations of the federal government.

a. Policy making

The President executes the laws — he cannot make them. But the President has some discretion in executing the laws, and he makes policy when exercising that discretion. In his concurrence to ***Youngstown Sheet & Tube Co. v. Sawyer***, 343 U.S. 579 (1952), Justice Jackson laid out a continuum for judging the constitutionality of presidential policy making in the domestic realm. That three-part continuum depends on the position that Congress takes with regard to his actions:

1) **The President acts with the express or implied approval of Congress:** When the President acts with the approval of Congress, his actions have the highest presumption of constitutionality. His actions are constitutional unless the Constitution expressly states that what he is doing is solely a function of Congress, or unless his actions go beyond the powers of the federal government as a whole.

   Example: The President cannot ratify a treaty because the Constitution expressly states that ratifying treaties is a function of the Senate.

   Example: Even if Congress authorized him to do so, the President could not issue an Executive Order declaring the legal standard for divorce in Ohio, because no arm of the federal government has the power to alter state family law.

2) **The President acts and Congress neither approves nor disapproves:** When Congress is silent about the President's actions, it is most difficult to determine the constitutionality of those actions. Courts will generally attempt to determine whether or not the silence amounts to approval or disapproval.

   Example: Congress passes a law governing labor relations and rejects an amendment that would give the President the power to seize heavy industries in the event of a national emergency. Five years later, the President declares a state of emergency and seizes the steel mills to prevent a strike. He requests Congress's approval but Congress does not respond. The Court decided that the later silence amounted to disapproval in light of Congress's refusal to give the President similar powers only five years prior to the seizure.

3) **The President acts and Congress disapproves:** When Congress disapproves of a President's actions, those actions are presumed to be unconstitutional. His actions are unconstitutional unless the President's actions fall within the President's inherent constitutional authority.

Example: Congress enacts an appropriations bill that mandates that the Interior Secretary spend $200 million to renovate facilities in the national parks. The President, citing fiscal concerns, declares that he will refuse to spend that money. The President's refusal to spend that money is presumed to be unconstitutional and he lacks the power to do so unless he has the inherent constitutional authority to refuse to spend money as part of his role in executing the laws. The Court would probably not agree that the President has inherent authority, so his refusal to spend the money is probably unconstitutional.

b. **Appointment of Executive Officials (Article II, § 2)**
The President appoints officials in the executive branch, but his power to do so is not absolute. Although Congress cannot itself appoint executive officials, it also plays a role in the appointments process. The amount of influence that Congress has over executive appointments depends on whether the executive official is a **principal** or **inferior** official.

The President has the **sole** power to appoint **principal** executive officials. However, appointments of principal officials must be approved by a majority of the Senate.

In contrast, Congress may decide who appoints **inferior** executive officials. Congress may vest this power in the President, the judicial branch, or in heads of departments. Interbranch appointments, such as joint appointments by the Attorney General and a court, are constitutionally permissible. ***Morrison v. Olson,*** 487 U.S. 654 (1988).

There is no bright line between principal and inferior officials. Cabinet officials and heads of departments are principal officials; generally, inferior officials are those officials who are supervised by principal officials. For example, in ***Morrison v. Olson,*** the Court held the independent prosecutor to be an inferior official because he could be removed by the Attorney General and had limited responsibilities, jurisdiction, and tenure.

c. **Removal of Executive Officials**
Generally, the President has the sole power to remove of executive officials, and he can do so at will. ***Meyers v. United States,*** 272 U.S. 52 (1926). Congress cannot itself remove executive officials, and it cannot place restrictions on executive officials who perform solely executive functions. When executive officials work for independent agencies or perform functions that are quasi-executive, Congress can place restrictions on the ability of the President to remove them from office as long as those restrictions do not substantially interfere with the President running the office. For example, in ***Humphrey's Executor v. United States,*** 295 U.S. 602 (1935), the Court held that Congress could limit the ability of the President to remove the head of the Federal Trade Commission because the FTC was an independent agency.

In ***Bowsher v. Synar,*** 478 U.S. 714 (1986), the Court considered the constitutionality of the Balanced Budget Act of 1985, which gave significant executive responsibilities to the Comptroller General, given that Congress could remove the Comptroller General by a joint resolution of Congress. The Court held the statute to be unconstitutional because Congress cannot remove an executive official short of impeaching him. The arrangement allowed Congress to exercise too much power over an executive official and thus violated principles of separation of powers.

d. Pardoning Power

Under Article II, § 2, the President has sweeping power to pardon criminal offenses, power that cannot be limited by Congress. The President may pardon a class of people by granting amnesty, or he may pardon an individual at any time subsequent to an offense, even prior to indictment. The power to pardon is not limited by doctrines against conflict of interest. The only limit to the President's pardoning power is that he may not pardon in cases of impeachment, and he may not pardon in anticipation of an offense.

Watch Out!

The pardoning power is confined to ***federal*** crimes. It does not extend to state law crimes.

e. Veto Power

Under Article I, § 7, legislation that has been approved by both Houses of Congress is presented to the President for his signature before it becomes law. The President must act within 10 days after the legislation is presented to him, and he has three choices.

1) **He may sign the bill into law.**

2) **He may veto the bill.** If he vetoes the bill, it is returned to Congress, and the bill can only become law if Congress overrides the veto by a two-thirds majority vote of both houses.

3) **He may do nothing.** If the President does nothing, then the bill becomes a law after 10 days, with the following exception of the "pocket veto." If adjournment of Congress (of 10 days or more) prevents the President from being able to veto a bill and return it to Congress, the President must sign the bill in order for it to become law. Under those circumstances, his failure to sign the bill is an absolute veto that cannot be overridden, known as a "pocket veto."

Line Item Veto Unconstitutional

In response to the enormous budget deficit at the end of the twentieth century, Congress enacted a Line Item Veto Act, which allowed the President to sign an appropriations bill into law and then decide not to spend certain items in that appropriations bill. In ***Clinton v. New York,*** 524 U.S. 417 (1998), the Court held the Act to be unconstitutional because it gave too much power to the President. Not only was the line item veto substantially different from the veto authorized in the Constitution, the Court said that the Act unconstitutionally gave the President the power to unilaterally alter the text of an enacted statute and thus violated separation-of-powers principles.

2. **Foreign Affairs Power**

In the realm of foreign affairs, the President is both the chief diplomat and the commander in chief of the armed forces. In these capacities, he is both the originator and spokesman of the country's foreign policy. Therefore the President has extremely broad power in the area of foreign affairs. The ability of Congress to delegate foreign affairs power to the executive branch is virtually unlimited. Moreover, the President has very few limits on what he can do with those powers.

The constitutionality of the President's foreign policy making is measured by the same tripartite continuum as that applied to domestic policy. However, in the realm of foreign affairs the President is given considerably more deference than in the domestic realm, with Congressional silence more likely to be interpreted as Congressional approval of the President's actions. For example, in ***Dames & Moore v. Regan***, 453 U.S. 654 (1981), the Court upheld the ability of the President to nullify attachments of property belonging to the Iranian government, and transfer all claims against the government of Iran to an international claims tribunal. The power to nullify attachments had been given to the President pursuant to statute, but the power to transfer claims had not. Nonetheless, the Court held that the power to transfer claims was the type of power that Congress intended to give to the President, construing Congressional silence as approval of the President's actions.

Although only Congress can declare war, the President can commit troops to battle without declaring war and has done so a number of times in the past half century. Congress's War Powers Act attempted to limit the President's ability to commit troops absent a declaration of war by requiring Congressional oversight and consent, but subsequent Presidents have consistently denied the constitutionality of that Act and the Court has yet to rule on it.

Although Congress must ratify any treaty before it becomes valid, the President may enter into executive agreements, which have a binding effect similar to treaties, without Congressional approval. The Court has upheld those agreements even when they authorized the seizure of private property. For example, when the President formally recognized the Soviet Union, he entered into an executive agreement to take over property located within the United States, which had been owned by Russians, on behalf of the Soviet Union. The underlying agreement and the seizure of property were found to be constitutional uses of the President's foreign powers in the case of ***United States v. Belmont,*** 301 U.S. 324 (1937). Similarly, the President's power to freeze attachments and transfer claims pursuant to an executive agreement was upheld in the case of ***Dames & Moore v. Regan,*** discussed above.

3. **Executive Privilege**
In ***United States v. Nixon,*** 418 U.S. 683 (1974), the Court held that the President enjoys a presumptive privilege for all of his communications, which protects him from disclosing them to a court. However, in most matters this privilege is not absolute. The President only enjoys an absolute privilege for communications regarding military, diplomatic, and national security matters.

In all other matters, the presumptive privilege must be weighed against the needs for fair administration of criminal justice — a generalized interest in confidentiality is not enough. In ***United States v. Nixon,*** for example, the Court ordered President Nixon to turn over tapes of his conversations with John Mitchell (his attorney general) when Mitchell was prosecuted for conspiracy to obstruct justice. The presumption of executive privilege was inadequate to outweigh the Court's need for administration of justice in that case.

4. **Executive Immunity**
The President is absolutely immune from civil suits for damages regarding his official acts. The Court established this immunity in the case of ***Nixon v. Fitzgerald***, 457 U.S. 731 (1982), when it ruled that a Pentagon whistle blower could not sue President Nixon for firing him in retaliation for his testimony before Congress regarding the abuse of funds by the military. The Court held that immunity for the President's official acts was justified in order to protect his decision making from being influenced by fear of suit, and to protect his time and other resources from being spent defending himself.

The Court was considerably less deferential to the President in the case of ***Clinton v. Jones,*** 520 U.S. 681 (1997), where the President claimed partial immunity in a suit for sexual harassment that allegedly occurred before he was elected president. The Court held that immunity for unofficial acts was not justified to protect Presidential decision making, and downplayed the burden on the president's time that such suits might create. The Court refused to find any Presidential immunity for unofficial acts, and denied the President's request to delay the lawsuit until after he would leave office.

5. **Federal Regulatory Power**
The administrative agencies that comprise much of the Executive Branch have vast regulatory powers. The agencies may issue rules and regulations as long as they are authorized to do so by Congress. In addition, administrative agencies may hold hearings and rule on individual compliance with the rules and regulations of those agencies, individual eligibility for federal programs, etc. Determinations of administrative agencies are entitled to deference by the courts.

a. Non-Delegation Doctrine
Congress has wide latitude to delegate policy making authority to executive agencies, and may delegate legislative power and discretion as long as it does so with an "intelligible principle" to which the administrative agency must conform. This is an extremely loose standard, and the Supreme Court has only struck down Congressional delegation of authority twice, in two 1935 cases.

b. Deference to Administrative Agency

An administrative agency is presumed to have expertise in the areas that it regulates, and a federal agency's construction of the statute it administers is entitled to a high degree of deference by the courts. The administrative agency determines how much policy making authority Congress intended to give that agency, and such determinations will be accepted by reviewing courts as long as the agency's interpretation is reasonable. All regulations issued by administrative agencies are entitled to this deference.

D. STATE POWERS IN AREAS OF FEDERAL AUTHORITY

State or local laws may run afoul of federal power in one of two ways: (a) **preemption** under the Supremacy Clause; or (b) violation of the **"dormant"** Commerce Clause. If Congress HAS legislated in the area, the question is whether the federal law **PREEMPTS** the state or local law. But even if Congress has NOT acted or NO preemption is found, the state or local law can be challenged on **DORMANT COMMERCE CLAUSE** grounds if it excessively burdens interstate commerce. In the sections immediately below, we discuss the Dorman Commerce Clause and then federal preemption under the Supremacy Clause.

1. The Dormant Commerce Clause

Only the federal government can regulate foreign and interstate commerce because of its national nature. But even when Congress chooses not to regulate, states are sharply limited in regulating interstate commerce. The "dormant" Commerce Clause prohibits states from discriminating against interstate commerce or placing undue burdens upon it.

a. How To Analyze a Dormant Commerce Clause Case

First, ask yourself: **"Does the state statute discriminate against out-of-staters?"**

A statute will be deemed discriminatory not only if it discriminates ***on its face*** but also if it has a discriminatory ***purpose*** or ***effect***. Look for protectionist legislation that treats in-state businesses more favorably than out-of-state businesses.

TEST #1: If the statute is discriminatory, it will be upheld only if it is ***necessary***, and employs the ***least restrictive means***, to achieve an ***important*** governmental purpose, a slight variation of the strict scrutiny test. The Supreme Court has stressed that this test is "virtually" a "per se rule of invalidity." ***Granholm v. Heald,*** 544 U.S. 460, 476 (2005).

Example of a discriminatory law: A state law restricted the price of milk that was produced out of state and prevented out-of-state milk from being sold at a price lower than in-state milk. ***Baldwin v. G.A.F. Seelig, Inc.,*** 294 U.S. 511 (1935).

Another example of a discriminatory law: Michigan allowed its in-state wineries to sell wine directly to Michigan consumers, but it prohibited out-of-state wineries from doing so. The Supreme Court struck the law down because it discriminated against interstate commerce, observing: "The mere fact of nonresidence should not foreclose a producer in one State from access to markets in other States." ***Granholm***

v. Heald, 544 U.S. 460, 472 (2005).

What if the state law is ***not*** discriminatory, but instead treats in-staters and out-of-staters alike? Here the Court uses a balancing test…

TEST #2: It will invalidate a state or local law under the Dormant Commerce Clause if its burden on interstate commerce exceeds its benefits.

Example of a non-discriminatory law: A state law required that all trucks within or passing through the state had to use *curved* mudguards — even though *straight* mudguards were legal in 45 other states and curved mudguards were prohibited in one other state. ***Bibb v. Navajo Freight Lines,*** 359 U.S. 520 (1959). Though non-discriminatory laws are frequently upheld under the foregoing balancing test (TEST #2), that test was used in ***Bibb*** to strike down the mudguard law.

b. Market participant exception

When the state acts as a market participant and chooses to conduct business only with in-state businesses, the state's decision to favor the in-state businesses does not violate the Dormant Commerce Clause. This exception applies regardless of whether the state is purchasing products from in-state producers, or selling products to in-state purchasers during shortages of that product.

2. State Taxation of Foreign and Interstate Commerce

a. State Taxation of Interstate Commerce

A state's ability to tax interstate commerce is limited both by the Dormant Commerce Clause and the Due Process Clause. In order for a state to tax interstate commerce, the tax must meet the following requirements:

1) **The tax must apply to an activity having a substantial nexus with the taxing state.**

A state may require out-of-state businesses to pay only taxes that are rationally related to local activities substantial enough to warrant compensation to the state. In addition, due process requires that the activity must have "minimum contacts" with the state and the person, thing, or transaction taxed.

Example: A state can only tax the profits of a corporation that are attributable to the corporation's business activities within the state. Generally, a state may not compel out-of-state businesses to pay sales tax unless the business sold and delivered goods within the state.

2) **The tax must be fairly apportioned.**

This requirement is designed to avoid the burden of cumulative taxation on an interstate business. A state tax on interstate commerce must be both internally and externally consistent.

Internal consistency: A tax is internally consistent if imposition of such a tax by every other state would not impose a higher burden on interstate commerce than that borne by intrastate commerce.

Example: A state registration fee for trucks is internally consistent because the truck driver only has to pay one registration fee; its registration is recognized by other states. On the other hand, a flat axle tax was not internally consistent because the driver might be required to pay such a tax in every state that he entered.

External consistency: A tax is externally consistent if the tax does not exceed the value fairly attributable to activity conducted within the taxing state.

Example: Retail sales taxes are externally consistent because only goods sold within the state are taxed.

3) **The tax must not discriminate against interstate commerce**

Example: A state cannot impose a higher tax on imported cement than that which was produced locally. Similarly, a state cannot give a property tax exemption to charities that serve solely local clientele and deny it to charities that serve out-of-state clients.

The requirement of nondiscrimination also prohibits taxes that do not discriminate on their face, but have the effect of burdening out-of-state enterprises more heavily than local enterprises.

Example: Taxes on door-to-door solicitation of orders for goods to be delivered later are unconstitutional because these types of sales are typically undertaken by out-of-state businesses.

4) **The tax must be fairly related to services provided by the state.**
This is a minimal requirement that the state provide *some* service to the business that it taxed, such as the maintenance of an infrastructure.

Example: If the state provides police service, fire service, mass transit, and other services that *could* be used by the business or its employees, the tax is considered fairly related to services provided by the state.

Although all four requirements must be met to withstand scrutiny, the most important of the four requirements is the requirement of non-discrimination.

b. Compensatory Use Taxes
A state tax that appears to be discriminatory on its face may still be constitutional if it is designed to make interstate commerce bear a burden already borne by intrastate commerce. Such a tax is known as a compensatory use tax. It is constitutional so

long as the taxing state identifies the intrastate tax for which it seeks to compensate, it does not exceed the amount of tax on the intrastate activity, and the taxes are imposed on substantially equivalent events.

Example: A state tax on the use of tangible personal property within a state, that exempted property the sale or use of which had already been taxed at an equal or higher rate by the state, was found to be constitutional because the burden the tax placed on goods purchased out of state was the same as that placed on in-state purchases.

c. State Taxation of Foreign Commerce

States are limited in taxing foreign commerce for the same reasons that they are limited in their ability to tax interstate commerce. Courts evaluating taxes on foreign commerce apply the same test as that for interstate commerce, with the requirements applying even more stringently. In addition, courts take two more factors into account when evaluating taxes on foreign commerce:

1) **Whether the tax enhances the risk of multiple taxation by foreign sovereigns**;

2) **Whether the tax might impair federal uniformity in this area so intimately connected with foreign relations.**

Example: The Court struck down a state tax on shipping containers that had arrived from Japan. The containers had already been taxed in Japan, and were subject to an international treaty on containers which had been signed by both Japan and the United States.

d. Import-Export Clause

The Import-Export Clause (Article I, § 10) prohibits states from taxing goods that are imported or exported in overseas commerce. When the clause applies, it absolutely prohibits state or local taxes. However, the tax only applies to goods that are still in transit. Once they have arrived at their destination, the state can levy property taxes on them.

Example: A large shipment of furniture from a factory in China to a wholesaler in Ohio passes through the state of New York while it is still in transit. It arrives in Ohio and is taken out of its boxes and stored in a warehouse. New York cannot levy a tax on the furniture in transit, but Ohio can impose an inventory tax on the furniture stored in the warehouse.

3. Federal Preemption of State Law

General: According to the Supremacy Clause (Article VI, clause 2), federal law is supreme. Therefore, as long as Congress has acted within an area delegated to it, federal law preempts all state regulation of that area. The intent of Congress is key to determining whether a state law is preempted by a federal statute. Courts are hesitant to find preemption unless Congressional intent to do so is clear, and tend to read Congressional purpose narrowly to avoid conflict with state law.

a. Express Preemption

Congress expressly preempts state regulation when it declares its intention to preclude state regulation of a federal area. The state is then prohibited from regulating in that area.

Example: A federal statute governing employee pensions and benefits expressly states that Congress intends to preempt any state regulation of employees' pensions and benefits. All state regulations of pensions and benefits are expressly preempted by that statute, including all state common-law and state statutory causes of action. ***Aetna Health Inc. v. Davila,*** 542 U.S. 200 (2004).

The Supreme Court recently embraced a broad conception of federal preemption, barring liability suits against the manufacturers of medical devices that have received "pre-market" approval from the Food and Drug Administration ("FDA"). ***Riegel v. Medtronic, Inc.***, 128 S. Ct. 999 (2008). In ***Riegel***, a cardiac patient sued the manufacturer of a balloon catheter that burst during his heart surgery after the doctor repeatedly inflated it beyond its labeled rupture point. The plaintiff asserted a number of state common-law tort claims against the manufacturer, but the Supreme Court rejected those claims, holding that they were preempted. In deciding this case, the Court was required to interpret a preemption clause in the federal statute that governs FDA pre-market approval of medical devices. The balloon catheter that burst in this case received the requisite pre-market approval. The applicable preemption clause does not *expressly* preempt common-law claims that challenge the safety or effectiveness of medical devices receiving pre-market approval. Instead, the preemption clause provides that States cannot impose any additional "requirement[s]" upon the manufacturers of devices that have won pre-market approval. State-imposed "requirement[s]," held the Court, include making the manufacturer liable for damages under state tort law.

b. Conflict Preemption

When a state law conflicts with a federal statute or its purpose, it is preempted by that federal law. A state law is preempted whenever compliance with both state and federal regulations is physically impossible or state law is a barrier to the accomplishment of a federal purpose. However, if it is possible to comply with both state and federal law, then conflict preemption does not apply.

Example: A federal regulation governing workplace safety requires the use of gloves when handling chemicals. A state regulation requires the use of goggles when handling chemicals but prohibits the use of gloves when handling chemical X. The regulation prohibiting the use of gloves when handling chemical X is preempted because it is impossible to comply with both federal and state regulations. However, the state regulation requiring the wearing of goggles is not preempted because it ***is*** possible to comply with both.

c. Field Preemption
Federal regulation of a field may preempt all state regulation in that area when it is clear that the federal government intended exclusively to regulate the entire field. Field preemption will be found when:

1) The federal scheme of regulation is **so pervasive** that the reasonable inference is that Congress left no room to supplement it; OR

2) The federal interest is **so dominant** that the federal system is assumed to preclude state regulation; OR

3) The **object** sought to be enforced and the **character of obligations** imposed by it reveal the same purpose.

Example: A state wrongful discharge action requiring the interpretation of a labor contract's union security clause was preempted because of the pervasiveness of federal regulation of labor-management relations.

4. State Sovereignty Limits on Federal Regulation
Over the past 20 years, the Court has limited the ability of the federal government to regulate based on principles of state sovereignty. These limits stem from the Tenth Amendment's protection of state sovereignty in general, and the sovereign immunity of states that is protected by the Eleventh Amendment.

a. State Sovereignty and Autonomy — The Tenth Amendment
The federal government has broad power to regulate states, but it is limited by principles of state sovereignty and autonomy. The federal government may regulate the states directly, including setting the hours and working conditions of state employees. ***Garcia v. San Antonio Metropolitan Transit Authority***, 469 U.S. 528 (1985). In addition, the federal government may impose federal standards on states by offering the states the choice between total federal preemption and allowing states to regulate according to those federal standards. ***New York v. United States***, 505 U.S. 144 (1992). But principles of state sovereignty prevent the federal government from "commandeering" state officials to perform federal functions. For example, in ***New York v. United States***, the Court held unconstitutional a federal statute requiring state legislatures to "take title" to radioactive waste if they refused to regulate such waste in strict accordance with federal dictates. The Court held that this statute unduly interfered with state legislative autonomy.

Federal commandeering of state government officials is prohibited regardless of whether those officials are members of the state legislature or executive branch officials. In ***Printz v. United States***, 521 U.S. 898 (1997), the Court held unconstitutional the portion of the Brady Handgun Violence Control Act which temporarily required county sheriffs to perform a national background check on would-be purchasers of handguns. The Court stated that the law was an unconstitutional commandeering of local law enforcement officials to act as an arm of the federal government.

b. State Sovereign Immunity — The Eleventh Amendment

1) **Issue-Spotting Advice:**
If you are confronted with a fact pattern in which Congress enacts a statute allowing private lawsuits against state governments (be on the lookout, in particular, for any federally-created cause of action that is used by a state employee to sue the state government that employs her), you are probably looking at an Eleventh Amendment issue.

2) **Black-Letter Rules:**

a) States are immune from suit for violating federal legislation enacted by Congress under its Article I powers.

b) This is true regardless of where they are sued — in state or federal court.

c) Congress can subject states to suit only through legislation that is grounded upon its Section 5 enforcement powers under the Fourteenth Amendment.

d) For state sovereign immunity to be abrogated, Congress must expressly invoke its Section 5 enforcement powers and make absolutely clear that it intends to subject the states to suit. Moreover, the legislation must qualify as a valid exercise of legislative power under the Fourteenth Amendment.

e) Eleventh Amendment sovereign immunity does not extend to lesser governmental entities like municipalities.

f) Eleventh Amendment sovereign immunity does not bar actions against state officers for injunctive or declaratory relief.

5. Relations Among States

a. Interstate Compacts
The Interstate Compact Clause (Article I, § 10, clause 3) prohibits states from entering into agreements or compacts with other states without the consent of Congress. The Court has interpreted this requirement loosely, easily finding Congressional consent to such agreements. Congressional consent may be inferred from a pattern or practice of enactments, prior authorization or subsequent approval, and may be conditioned on state acceptance of Congressional modifications.

Example: The Court upheld an agreement between Connecticut and Massachusetts to allow bank holding companies from other New England states (and no other states) to do business in those states as long as the holding company's home state extended reciprocal privileges. The Court held that Congress had authorized such agreements in the Bank Holding Company Act.

b. Full Faith and Credit

The Full Faith and Credit Clause (Article IV, § 1) requires states to recognize legal relationships created by governments of other states. Thus, a judgment entered into by a court in State A is enforceable in State B. Similarly, state B is required to recognize the marriage of a couple married in State A in accordance with the law of State A.

Watch Out!

SAME-SEX MARRIAGE UNDER THE FULL FAITH AND CREDIT CLAUSE

The controversy over same-sex marriage has prompted some courts to recognize limits on the extent to which a state must honor the Full Faith and Credit Clause when it comes to recognizing same-sex unions performed in other states. Though the U.S. Supreme Court has yet to decide this question definitively, some lower courts are recognizing a "public policy" exception to the Full Faith and Credit Clause. See, e.g., ***Wilson v. Ake,*** 354 F. Supp. 2d 1298 (M.D. Fla. 2005) (Full Faith and Credit Clause does not require a state to apply another state's law in violation of its own legitimate public policy) (holding that Florida was not required to recognize lesbian marriage legally performed in Massachusetts).

E. INDIVIDUAL RIGHTS

1. State or Governmental Action Requirement

General Rule: The individual rights guaranteed by the Constitution are generally only enforceable against the state or a state actor. A state actor is usually a government employee or agency, but some private parties are considered to be state actors if they have close enough ties to the government. In determining whether a private party can be considered a state actor, look to his activity to determine whether it is governmental in nature, or whether there is a strong enough nexus between the private actors and the state.

a. Governmental Function

If a private actor is performing a government function, it may be considered to be a state actor. It is not enough that the function be one that has historically been performed by the state — it must be a function that has **exclusively** been reserved to the state and that is generally associated with state sovereignty. This test is generally applied restrictively and rarely leads to a finding of state action.

Example: A privately-owned company town was found to be a state actor because the owner who ran the town performed the function of a city government — a function that has historically been exclusively reserved to the government. On the other hand, a public utility company was not a state actor, even though its activities strongly affected the public interest, because operating public utilities has not historically been a function exclusively performed by the state.

Watch Out!

Company towns are a thing of the past. So you won't likely encounter them on the Bar Exam. But there is a new phenomenon that is generating state action litigation in the lower courts: publicly funded sports complexes featuring a stadium and/or arena that are run by a private corporation specifically formed to manage the complex.

If public officials dominate the private corporation's board of directors, the corporation may be deemed a state actor under the "Symbiotic Relationship" doctrine (see below). If public sidewalks ringing the complex merge imperceptibly with the complex's private sidewalks, and the corporation performs the public function of regulating public access to its sidewalks, the corporation may be deemed a state actor under the "Governmental Function" doctrine. ***United Church of Christ v. Gateway Economic Development Corp.,*** 383 F.3d 449, 454-55 (6th Cir. 2004) (holding that private operator of stadium-arena complex in Cleveland was a state actor when regulating protesters on its sidewalks).

b. Private and Public "Symbiotic Relationships"

When the state is involved in a private activity to "some significant extent," the private actor may be found to be a state actor. For example, if the private involvement is necessary for the public entity to continue to function, or vice versa, there exists a symbiotic relationship that makes that private actor into a state actor. This test is also applied narrowly — the public and private activity must be very closely related for a court to find state action. However, joint participation between a private party and a state official is state action if the private party's action is fairly attributable to the state.

Example: When a publicly-owned parking garage paid for most of its operating expenses with lease money paid by a private restaurant, the owner of that restaurant was found to be a state actor. When a clerk issued an attachment writ as part of an ex parte proceeding to attach the debtor's property initiated by a private party, the clerk's involvement was sufficient to meet the symbiotic relationship test.

1) Judicial Enforcement of Private Action

Judicial enforcement of a racially restrictive covenant was found to be sufficient state involvement to make the property owners attempting to enforce those covenants into state actors. This ruling has since been narrowed by the Court, and it may apply only to situations where the state intervention has the effect of blocking a transaction between a seller and a buyer.

2) Government Licensing and Regulation
Even though a private business might require a state license to operate, that state license does not make the private business into a state actor. Nor does extensive state regulation of a business satisfy the requirement of a symbiotic relationship.
Example: A private bar required a state liquor license to operate. Neither the license itself, nor the state regulation incident to the provision of that license, is sufficient to make the bar into a state actor.

c. State Encouragement of Private Action
When the state actively encourages private action, through policy or legislation, that private action may be considered to be state action. However, mere approval by a state commission does not constitute state action, even if that approval gives the private actor a monopoly over the services that it provides. The state must have either exercised **coercive power** or **significantly encouraged** the private activity.

Example: A privately owned nursing home that received 90% of its funding from the state was not found to be a state actor on the basis of state encouragement of private action. Even though the state funding supported the operations of the nursing home in general, the funding did not prove that the state had affirmatively commanded the **specific** activity (transfers of patients without due process of law) that formed the basis of the suit.

2. Federal Citizenship and Alienage:

a. Acquisition of Citizenship
United States citizenship may be acquired by birth or naturalization. Citizenship of a naturalized citizen is equal in every way to that of citizenship acquired by birthright.

1) Native Born Citizen
All persons born within the United States are citizens of the United States and the state in which they reside. In addition, a person born abroad is a citizen of the United States if one parent was a U.S. citizen and he or she lived continuously in the United States for at least 5 years between the ages of 14 and 28.

2) Naturalized Citizen
Congress plays a sweeping role in determining the requirements for naturalized citizenship and the process by which citizenship is acquired or lost — and the requirements set by Congress are not judicially reviewable.

In order to become a naturalized citizen, a person must have been a lawful resident of the United States for 5 years (or 3 years if he or she is married to a United States citizen), have good moral character, exhibit attachment to the principles of the Constitution, and exhibit some ability to read in English.

b. Loss of Citizenship
Citizenship cannot be taken away — it must be relinquished voluntarily.

Example: The Court has struck down a federal law which purported to withdraw citizenship from citizens who voted in foreign elections, and a law which purported to withdraw citizenship from citizens who lived outside of the country for more than three years in nations to which they formerly held allegiance. Both laws violated the principle that citizenship can only be relinquished voluntarily.

c. Status of Aliens

Congress determines the standards by which the entry, stay, and naturalization of aliens are to be determined. However, an alien is considered to be a "person" protected by the Equal Protection Clause of the Fourteenth Amendment and therefore cannot be discriminated against by state governments on the basis of alienage.

3. Privileges and Immunities of National Citizenship

a. Introduction

The privileges and immunities of national citizenship are those rights "which owe their existence to the Federal government, its National character, its Constitution or its laws." ***The Slaughter-House Cases***, 83 U.S. (16 Wall.) 36, 79 (1873). Over the years, the Court has identified the following privileges or immunities:

1) **The right to travel.**

2) **The right to vote** in federal elections.

3) **The right to petition** the federal government and inform United States officials about violations of its laws.

4) **The right to enter** national lands.

5) **The right to protection** when under the custody of a United States Marshal.

b. Two different clauses

There are two discrete clauses in the Constitution that refer to "privileges" and "immunities":

1) The Privileges AND Immunities Clause of Article IV, § 2; and

2) The Privileges OR Immunities Clause of the Fourteenth Amendment.

Each clause performs a distinct role. The former restricts the power of a state to discriminate against out-of-staters (i.e., American citizens residing in some other state) who seek to visit or do business in that state. The latter restricts the power of a state to discriminate against American citizens who have recently taken up residence in that state.

The key function of each clause implicates the so-called "right to travel." So before examining each clause separately, let's pause for a brief footnote on the right to travel.

c. A footnote on the "right to travel"

The right to travel has several different components. It includes not only the right to move freely from state to state, but also:

1) The right of an out-of-stater to be free from unreasonable discrimination while temporarily present in another state (this right is protected by the Privileges AND Immunities Clause of Article IV, § 2, per ***Saenz v. Roe***, 526 U.S. 489, 500-01 (1999)); and

2) The right of an out-of-stater, upon moving to a new state and taking up permanent residence there, to be treated equally vis-à-vis long-time residents of that state (this right is protected by the Privileges OR Immunities Clause of the Fourteenth Amendment, per ***Saenz v. Roe***, 526 U.S. 489, 502-03 (1999)).

   Of these two components, only the second is a ***fundamental*** right, to be analyzed under ***strict scrutiny***. As discussed below, violations of the first component are reviewed under a form of intermediate scrutiny.

   Bear in mind, finally, that the term "right to travel" is almost always used in reference to the ***second*** component identified above. Moreover, most of the Supreme Court cases dealing with the "right to travel" have involved durational residency requirements implicating that second component. Unless otherwise specified, any reference in these materials to the "right to travel" is meant to refer specifically to this ***second*** component.

d. The Privileges AND Immunities Clause of Article IV, § 2

The Supreme Court has interpreted this clause as limiting the ability of a state to discriminate against out-of-staters with regard to fundamental rights or important economic activities.

1) **Fundamental Rights:** The Court has held, for example, that a state cannot discriminate against out-of-staters in affording meaningful access to its courts, ***Canadian Northern Railway Co. v. Eggen***, 252 U.S. 553 (1920), or in limiting the ability of out-of-staters to obtain abortions in the state, ***Doe v. Bolton***, 410 U.S. 179 (1973).

2) **Important Economic Activities:** Most cases under the Privileges and Immunities Clause involve states discriminating against out-of-staters in ways that hinder their ability to earn their livelihood. The Supreme Court has found this clause to be violated if a state excludes out-of-staters from practicing a trade or profession, or charges a discriminatory licensing fee, or mandates that a preference be given to in-staters for employment. *See, e.g.,* ***Supreme Court of New Hampshire v. Piper***, 470 U.S. 274 (1985) (striking down a New Hampshire law that required residence in the

state in order to be admitted to the bar); ***Toomer v. Witsell***, 334 U.S. 385 (1948) (striking down a South Carolina law that required nonresidents to pay a license fee of $2,500 for each commercial shrimp boat, while residents only had to pay a fee of $25.27); *id.* at 403 ("[O]ne of the privileges which the clause guarantees to citizens of State A is that of doing business in State B on terms of substantial equality with citizens of that State.").

But the Privileges and Immunities Clause is not an absolute, and alleged violations of it are not analyzed under strict scrutiny. Instead, the Court employs a form of intermediate scrutiny, which it has articulated as follows: "The Clause does not preclude discrimination against nonresidents where: (i) there is a substantial reason for the difference in treatment; and (ii) the discrimination against nonresidents bears a substantial relationship to the State's objective. In deciding whether the discrimination bears a close or substantial relationship to the State's objective, the Court has considered the availability of less restrictive means." ***Supreme Court of New Hampshire v. Piper***, 470 U.S. 274, 284 (1985).

In applying this test, the Court has rejected claims under the Privileges and Immunities Clause if they did not involve discrimination against out-of-staters in the exercise of fundamental constitutional rights or the ability to earn a livelihood. Thus, in ***Baldwin v. Fish & Game Commission of Montana***, 436 U.S. 371 (1978), the Court upheld a Montana law that charged out-of-staters a much higher fee for elk hunting licenses than that required of in-staters. The Court explained that "[e]lk hunting by nonresidents in Montana is a recreation and a sport" — it is neither a constitutional right nor a means of earning a livelihood. 436 U.S. at 388.

e. The Privileges OR Immunities Clause of the Fourteenth Amendment

From the time of ***The Slaughter-House Cases***, 83 U.S. (16 Wall.) 36 (1873) until 1999, the Privileges or Immunities Clause of the Fourteenth Amendment was treated by the Supreme Court as affording individuals no protection from state governmental actions and furnishing federal courts with no basis to invalidate state laws. But suddenly and recently, the clause has come to life. In ***Saenz v. Roe***, 526 U.S. 489, 502-03 (1999), the Court identified the clause as the constitutional home for the "right to travel" — and, for only the second time in 133 years, it used the clause to strike down a state law.

For purposes of this clause, the right to travel is the right to be free from discrimination upon moving to a state and taking up permanent residence there — the right to be treated equally vis-à-vis long-time residents of that state. This right used to be conceived as a component of the Equal Protection Clause. After ***Saenz***, the right is expressly identified with the Privileges or Immunities Clause — and its principal utility will be to invalidate durational residency requirements.

A durational residency requirement is where newly-arrived residents must live in the jurisdiction for a specified period of time in order to receive a benefit that long-time residents are afforded. Examples include waiting periods required for receipt of welfare benefits, voting, and divorces.

For "right to travel" purposes, there is an important difference between residency requirements and ***durational*** residency requirements. Only the ***latter*** violate the Privileges or Immunities Clause, and only the ***latter*** are subject to strict scrutiny. Residency requirements, on the other hand, are best challenged under the Privileges AND Immunities Clause of Article IV, § 2, and are analyzed under the intermediate scrutiny test outlined above.

What is the difference between residency requirements and durational residency requirements? Residency requirements provide a benefit to ***all current residents***, no matter how long they have lived in the state, that is not available to nonresidents. By contrast, durational residency requirements draw a distinction among current residents based on how long they have resided in the state. The Supreme Court has recognized that durational residency requirements discourage interstate travel, especially migration. Accordingly, the Court has held that durational residency requirements must be analyzed under strict scrutiny.

Saenz v. Roe held that state welfare programs may not restrict new residents to the level of welfare benefits they would have received in the state from which they moved. It struck down a California law that established such a two-tiered benefit scheme, concluding that it violated the "right to travel" protected by the Privileges or Immunities Clause of the Fourteenth Amendment. 526 U.S. at 502-03.

In the wake of ***Saenz***, you should apply STRICT SCRUTINY to any state law that impinges upon this right to travel, 526 U.S. at 504, and you should invoke the Privileges or Immunities Clause of the Fourteenth Amendment, NOT the Equal Protection Clause, when confronted with any right-to-travel scenario.

In the aftermath of ***Saenz***, how will courts analyze the constitutionality of in-state tuition preferences for public universities? Differences between in-state and out-of-state tuition are often significant. The key will likely be whether the scheme merely prefers in-state residents to out-of-staters (a scenario that implicates the Privileges AND Immunities Clause, warranting only intermediate scrutiny), or whether this preference is imposed by means of a ***durational*** residency requirement (which, after ***Saenz***, would implicate the Privileges OR Immunities Clause, requiring ***strict*** scrutiny). The Court has recognized that a residency requirement for lower tuition would be constitutional because "a State has a legitimate interest in protecting and preserving ... the right of its own bona fide residents to attend [its colleges and universities] on a preferential tuition basis." ***Vlandis v. Kline***, 412 U.S. 441, 452-53 (1973). But the Court struck down a law that permanently precluded out-of-state applicants from ever receiving in-state tuition, even if they moved to the state right after applying and established residency there. *Id.* One commentator has observed that, in the wake of ***Saenz***, "courts will have to decide whether in-state tuition preferences impermissibly prefer longer-term residents over newer ones, or whether such laws are permissible efforts by states to define when a person becomes a resident." ERWIN CHEMERINSKY, *CONSTITUTIONAL LAW: PRINCIPLES AND POLICIES* §10.7.2, at 868 (3d ed. 2006).

4. **Due Process**

The Due Process Clauses of the Fifth and Fourteenth Amendments prevent the government from taking property, liberty, or life from a person without providing them with due process of law. Due Process provides more than purely procedural protections — it also creates some substantive rights that cannot be infringed by the government.

a. **Procedural Due Process**

Procedural due process is based on the premise that the government should treat its citizens fairly. Due process protections only apply to intentional governmental action — they do not apply to unintentional acts such as governmental negligence. Procedural due process must be provided where: 1) there is a governmental deprivation of liberty or property to which the claimant is entitled; and 2) potential factual issues exist which affect an individual or small group as opposed to the public at large.

These protections apply only to individuals or groups that are affected by a governmental decision, and do not apply to governmental action that affects the public at large. For example, in ***Bi-Metallic Investment Co. v. State Board of Equalization***, 239 U.S. 441 (1915), the Court ruled that taxpayers were not entitled to a hearing before the Board of Equalization imposing an order increasing the value of all taxable property in Denver by 40 percent. By contrast, in ***Londoner v. Denver***, 210 U.S. 373 (1908), the Court held that individual property owners were entitled to hearings before the city assessed them for the cost of local improvements.

Courts follow a two-step process to determine the amount of process which is due. First, they determine whether there is a property, liberty or life interest at stake. The meaning of governmental deprivation of life is clear, but there has been much litigation over the existence of a property or liberty interest. Whether or not the claimant has a property or liberty interest is a threshold question — if the claimant has no such interest, then he is not entitled to any procedural protection. If he does have a property or liberty interest, then the next step is to determine how much process is due.

1) **Protected "Liberty" or "Property" Interests**

To have a protected property or liberty interest, a person must have a reasonable belief that he is entitled to that property or liberty. That person's unilateral expectation is not sufficient — the entitlement must be created by a separate source of law, such as a state statute or administrative rules. ***Roth v. Board of Regents***, 408 U.S. 564 (1971). The ***Roth*** ruling makes it appear that the state has the discretion to deny due process rights simply by stating that a person is not entitled to the liberty or property at stake, but the Court has never gone so far as finding that the government can deny a property interest simply by stating that it does not exist. Moreover, in ***Cleveland Board of Education v. Loudermill***, 470 U.S. 532 (1985), the Court expressly rejected the argument that a state may create any procedural limitations that it wishes in the process of creating a benefit.

Example: In, ***Roth***, the Court held that a tenure-track professor who merely expected to be renewed by his university employer did not have a property interest in his job, because his written contract expired on a certain date and there was no rule or policy supporting his unilateral expectation. By contrast, in ***Perry v. Sinderman***, 408 U.S. 593 (1972), the Court held that a tenure-track professor who works for a university with a faculty manual providing that professors will be retained as long as their work is satisfactory does have a property interest in his job.

The following are examples of ***property interests****:*

a) **Government benefits**. In ***Goldberg v. Kelly***, 397 U.S. 254 (1970), the Court held for the first time that government must provide notice and a hearing before terminating welfare benefits. The Court held that the claimants had a property interest in the welfare benefits because the federal law creating those benefits stated that all eligible people were entitled to the benefits. In ***Dandridge v. Williams***, 397 U.S. 471 (1970), the Court clarified that the entitlement status of the welfare benefits stemmed from the statutory language rather than an inherent right to welfare. Since the current statute creating welfare benefits states clearly that they are not an entitlement, it is unclear whether recipients are still entitled to due process protections. Although the Court has yet to rule on this issue, it is unlikely that it would find that no process was due welfare recipients, given the policy of fairness that lies behind due process protections.

b) **Government licenses**, such as driver's licenses or professional licenses.

c) **Government employment** if the employee has a reasonable expectation that her job will continue absent good cause for termination.

d) Receipt of a **public education**. The Court has held that suspension or expulsion of a student from a public school is a deprivation of liberty and property requiring due process.

e) **Public utility service** when state regulations state that the service can only be terminated for "good cause."

The following are examples of ***liberty interests****:*

a) **Constitutional rights** such as First Amendment protections and criminal procedure protections.

b) **Freedom from physical restraint**, including civil commitment for adults (but not for children being committed by their parents).

c) **Parental rights** including the right to custody of one's children but not including the right of an unmarried biological father when the mother was married to another man.

d) **Deportation and exclusion proceedings.**

e) **Liberty interests for prisoners:** The Court has examined state laws and prison regulations to determine whether there is a reasonable expectation of a liberty interest. More recently, however, the Court has held that prisoners only have a liberty interest when they are subject to a significant deprivation of freedom that is atypical to the usual conditions of confinement. This ruling appears to limit the extent to which statutes and regulations can create a liberty interest.

Liberty interests have been found in revocations of parole, revocation of probation, awards of "good time" credits, transfers from prisons to mental hospitals, and avoiding the administration of anti-psychotic medications. However, prisoners do not have a liberty interest in remaining in minimum-security, rather than maximum-security, facilities unless state law clearly creates an interest.

f) **Harm to reputation,** by itself, is not sufficient to create a liberty interest. However, due process is required if the harm to reputation is accompanied by deprivation of a tangible benefit, such as loss of a job.

2) What Process is Due

Once a court has determined that an individual is entitled to a liberty or property interest, the next step is to determine how much process is required before the government can take that interest away. **The basic elements of due process are notice of the charges or issue, a meaningful hearing, and an impartial decision maker.** ***Mullane v. Central Hannover Bank & Trust Co.***, 399 U.S. 306 (1950).

Elements

The basic elements of due process are:

1. **notice of the charges or issue**;
2. **a meaningful hearing**; and
3. **an impartial decisionmaker**.

However, there are many possible variations on these rights. For example, must the notice be personally served or is posting sufficient? Is a pre-deprivation hearing required, or is a post-deprivation hearing sufficient? Is a full trial-like adversarial hearing required, or is a less formal proceeding sufficient, and is the claimant entitled to have an attorney at the hearing?

In the case of ***Mathews v. Eldridge,*** 424 U.S. 319 (1976), the Court articulated a balancing test for determining the level of process that is due when there is a deprivation of a property or liberty interest. The ***Mathews*** Court identified three factors that must be balanced:

a) **The private interest that will be affected by the official action;**

b) **The risk of an erroneous deprivation of that interest; and**

c) **The probable value, if any, of substitute procedural safeguards and the administrative costs of providing those safeguards.**

The more important the private interest, the higher the risk of erroneous deprivation, and the higher the probable value of substitute safeguards, the more process that is due. However, all of these factors will be weighed against the cost of the procedure to the state, and in applying the ***Mathews*** test, the Court generally finds the cost to the state to be significant.

a) Government Benefits and Services

In ***Goldberg v. Kelly,*** 397 U.S. 254 (1970), the Court held that welfare beneficiaries were entitled to notice and a pre-deprivation hearing with procedural protections such as the right to call and cross-examine witnesses, and to have an attorney present. By contrast, the Court in ***Mathews*** held that Social Security recipients were only entitled to a post-deprivation hearing.

The ***Mathews*** Court held that Social Security recipients needed fewer protections because unlike welfare recipients, they did not depend on their benefits for their livelihood so the benefits were less important than in ***Goldberg***. Applying the second factor, determinations of eligibility for Social Security benefits are based primarily on medical records so there was a lower possibility of erroneous deprivation. And the Court held the likely cost of pre-termination hearings to be very high because recipients would exhaust all of their appeals while they continued to receive benefits.

Not surprisingly, since ***Mathews*** the Court has generally been satisfied with post-termination hearings than it was earlier. For example, before ***Mathews***, the Court had found that a pre-deprivation hearing was required before suspending a person's driving license, but after ***Mathews*** the Court held that a driver's license could be suspended before a hearing when the license was suspended because its owner refused to take a breathalyzer test. Similarly, in

Walters v. National Association of Radiation Survivors, 473 U.S. 305 (1985) the Court upheld a federal law limiting to $10 the amount of attorneys' fees that can be paid to attorneys who represent successful claimants for veterans benefits, and in ***United States Department of Labor v. Triplett***, 494 U.S. 715 (1990), the Court upheld a federal law prohibiting the collection of attorneys' fees for lawyers who represent successful claimants for Black Lung benefits unless the fees were approved by the Department of Labor or a court.

b) **Government Employees**
Applying the ***Mathews*** test to government employees, the Court has reached a compromise for government employees that are being fired. Pre-termination, government employees are only entitled to an informal review process. If necessary, the employee then has a right to a full hearing only after he has been terminated.

c) **Family Rights**
The Court's rulings on the amount of process due in cases involving parental rights. On the one hand, the Court has held that in order to terminate parental rights, the state must prove by "clear and convincing evidence" that such terminations are necessary, and has held that the state must pay for blood tests for indigent defendants in paternity cases. On the other hand, the Court held that the state is not required to provide an attorney for an indigent parent who is contesting the termination of her parental rights. State appointment of an attorney is only required when that parent also faces criminal charges in connection with the litigation.

d) **Educational Institutions**
The amount of process due to public school students facing suspension varies in accordance with the length of suspension. Thus, the Court has held that notice of the suspension and an opportunity to explain is sufficient for students facing short suspensions, while a more formal process is required for students facing longer suspensions or expulsion.

The Court tends to be deferential to educational institutions in cases involving the due process rights of students. For example, the Court has held that no process is required prior to the infliction of corporal punishment, and no hearing was required for a medical student who was dismissed because of perceived poor performance in her clinical classes. The Court held that placing the medical student on probation, evaluating her with a panel of seven doctors, and the approval of her dismissal by the dean and the president of the university were sufficient to satisfy due process.

e) **Children's Rights**
Children are generally entitled to fewer procedural rights than adults suffering the same deprivation. For example, adults facing involuntary civil commitment are entitled to notice and a hearing prior to commitment, but

children are not entitled to such protections when they are involuntarily committed by their parents.

f) Prisoners' Rights

The range of procedures required for prisoners varies in accordance with the Court's view of the significance of the liberty interest implicated. Thus, prisoners directly facing the loss of freedom in parole and probation revocation proceedings are entitled to a high level of procedural rights, whereas prisoners facing disciplinary action such as the revocation of good time credits are entitled to a lower level of procedure.

Prisoners are entitled to full hearings when their probation or parole is being revoked. At the preliminary hearing, they are entitled to notice of the alleged violation, an opportunity to appear and produce evidence, a conditional right to confront adverse witnesses, an independent decision-maker, and a written report of the proceedings. At a final hearing on revocation of parole or probation, a prisoner is entitled to even more protections, including disclosure of the evidence to be presented against him and a neutral and detached hearing body. On the other hand, the Court held that significantly less formal procedures, including no notice of the exact date of the hearing, were sufficient for determinations of eligibility for parole.

Prisoners are not entitled to the appointment of an attorney at revocation hearings, nor are they entitled to an attorney at proceedings revoking good time credit. By contrast, prisoners facing transfer from a prison to a state mental institution are entitled to full blown evidentiary hearings ***and*** the appointment of an attorney at those hearings. Finally, prisoners are entitled to a semi-formal hearing to contest the involuntary administration of anti-psychotic drugs.

g) "Enemy Combatants"

A citizen held in the United States as an "enemy combatant" has a due process right to notice of the factual basis for his classification. He also has a due process right to be given a meaningful opportunity to contest the factual basis for his classification before a neutral decision maker. ***Hamdi v. Rumsfeld***, 542 U.S. 507 (2004).

More recently, the Supreme Court ruled that aliens detained as enemy combatants at Guantánamo Bay were entitled to the privilege of habeas corpus to challenge the legality of their detention in federal court. ***Boumediene v. Bush***, 128 S. Ct. 2229 (2008).

h) Government Confiscation and Sale of a Person's Home for Nonpayment of Taxes

Before a State may take property and sell it for unpaid taxes, the Due Process Clause of the Fourteenth Amendment requires the government to provide the property owner with notice of the impending sale and an opportunity for a hearing. Due process does not require that the property owner receive actual notice. But when notice of a tax sale is mailed to the owner and returned undelivered, the Due Process Clause requires that the government "must take additional reasonable steps to attempt to provide notice to the property owner before selling his property." ***Jones v. Flowers,*** 547 U.S. 220, 225 (2006). Simply publishing a notice in the newspaper several weeks prior to the sale, without ever posting notice at the address to which notice was sent or taking other measures reasonably available to alert the seller, is constitutionally insufficient. *Id.* at 234-38.

b. Substantive Due Process

Although the language of the Due Process Clause itself refers only to procedural rights, the Supreme Court has also located some substantive rights in that clause. The doctrine of substantive due process protects a certain sphere of individual autonomy and liberty that cannot be taken away, or interfered with, by the government. When the state interferes with the rights protected by substantive due process, the Court balances the right against the state's interest in infringing on that right to determine the constitutionality of the state action.

Note: Before delving into the history and details of substantive due process, here are some materials that you should MEMORIZE in preparation for the Bar Exam:

1) There are two tests that govern substantive due process claims: **strict scrutiny** and **rational basis review**.
   a) Under strict scrutiny, the challenged regulation must be **necessary** to achieve a **compelling** governmental purpose.
   b) Under rational basis review, the regulation need only be **rationally** related to a **legitimate** governmental purpose.

2) Apply **strict scrutiny** if any of the following **fundamental rights** is implicated:
   a) The right to **bear and raise children** in accordance with one's beliefs.
   b) The right to **marry**.
   c) Access to **birth control**.
   d) The right to **refuse medical treatment**, even if that treatment is life-saving.
   e) The right to choose to have an **abortion** — restricted by ***Casey's*** "undue burden" standard.

3) In the context of substantive due process, the following are **not** fundamental rights; they are governed, accordingly, by **rational basis** review:
   a) The right to **assisted suicide**.
   b) Regulation in the **economic** realm after ***Lochner's*** downfall in 1937.

4) The right to engage in same-gender sex is not so easily categorized. As explained more fully ***infra***, state sodomy laws directed at same-gender sex are now flatly unconstitutional. ***Lawrence v. Texas***, 539 U.S. 558 (2003). But in arriving at that result, the Supreme Court did not expressly state whether there is a "fundamental

right" to engage in same-gender sex. Nor did it expressly apply strict scrutiny.

The Court first recognized the doctrine of substantive due process at the beginning of the twentieth century, in what is known as the "***Lochner*** era." In ***Lochner v. New York***, 198 U.S. 45 (1905) and a number of other cases, the Court found the freedom of contract to be encompassed in the liberty protected by the Due Process Clause of the Fourteenth Amendment. During the same era, the Court also read the concept of liberty broadly to encompass the non-economic rights "to engage in any of the common occupations of life, to acquire useful knowledge, to marry, establish a home and bring up children, to worship God in accordance with one's conscience, and generally to enjoy those privileges long recognized at common law as essential to the orderly pursuit of happiness by free men." ***Meyer v. Nebraska***, 262 U.S. 390 (1923).

The Court has long since rejected its ruling in ***Lochner*** and repudiated the concept of substantive due process in the economic realm. However, the Court continues to protect individual autonomy and liberty in a series of cases recognizing a "right to privacy." In ***Griswold v. Connecticut***, 381 U.S. 479 (1965), the Court first identified the right to privacy in the "penumbras" of various constitutional provisions, including the Due Process Clause and the First, Third, Fourth, Fifth, and Ninth Amendments, holding that the right to privacy protects the right of a married couple to choose to use birth control. After ***Griswold***, the Court extended the right to privacy to cover the right of unmarried individuals to use birth control, the right to choose to have an abortion, and the right to refuse medical treatment, including life support.

a) Locating Fundamental Rights

Fundamental rights are rights that are "implicit in the concept of ordered liberty," and "deeply rooted in our nation's history and tradition." ***Washington v. Glucksberg***, 521 U.S. 702, 720-21 (1997). Applying this test, the Court has found the following to be fundamental rights:

1. **The right to bear and raise children in accordance with one's beliefs.** For example, the Court struck down a state law that allowed for the sterilization of a man convicted of a felony involving "moral turpitude" as unduly infringing on one of the "basic civil rights of man." ***Skinner v. Oklahoma***, 316 U.S. 535 (1942). In ***Meyer***, the Court reversed the conviction of a teacher for teaching German and thus violating a law that prohibited teaching children a foreign language. And in ***Pierce v. Society of Sisters***, 268 U.S. 510 (1925), the Court upheld a challenge by parochial schools to an Oregon law requiring children to attend public school. This right extends to the decision one makes regarding the composition of one's family. In ***Moore v. East Cleveland***, 431 U.S. 494 (1977), the Court invalidated a zoning ordinance that limited occupancy of a dwelling to members of a single family and defined that family as including only a few categories of related individuals. The Court found that the ordinance

violated the fundamental right of the plaintiff, a grandmother who lived with two grandsons who were first cousins, to choose how to define her own family.

Example: The right to home school one's children falls under this category of fundamental rights.

2. **The right to marry.** In ***Zablocki v. Redhail***, 343 U.S. 374 (1978), the Court identified a fundamental "right to marry" when it struck down a Wisconsin law that prohibited anyone who was required to pay child support from marrying without court approval.

3. **The right of an individual, whether married or unmarried, to use birth control, and the right of a doctor to prescribe it.** In ***Griswold***, the Court struck down a Connecticut statute that made it illegal to use birth control, overturning the convictions of doctors who were found guilty as accessories to that use. The Court held that the statute violated the fundamental right of a married couple to use birth control. In ***Eisenstadt v. Baird***, 405 U.S. 438 (1972), the Court clarified that the right to use birth control was not limited to married couples when it struck down a law making it illegal to distribute birth control. The Court explained that the right to privacy protected the right of an "individual, married or single, to be free from unwarranted governmental intrusion into matters so fundamentally affecting a person as the decision whether to bear or beget a child."

4. **The right to choose to have an abortion**. In the controversial case of ***Roe v. Wade***, 410 U.S. 113 (1973), the Court held that an individual has a fundamental right to choose to have an abortion. Although the Court has limited that right in a number of cases, and has since rejected some of its reasoning in ***Roe***, the right to an abortion continues to be a fundamental right.

5. **The right to refuse medical treatment, even if that treatment is life saving.** In ***Cruzan v. Director, Missouri Dept. of Health***, 497 U.S. 261 (1990), the Court identified a fundamental right to refuse medical treatment, even if that treatment would save or prolong one's life. However, the Court would not extend that right to the family of a woman who had been in a coma for several years, surviving on life support systems. Because this right belongs to the individual patient, the Court upheld the Missouri law that required a showing of "clear and convincing evidence" that the patient herself would have wanted the life support systems to be turned off. The Court indicated that a living will or power of attorney might provide adequate evidence of intent.

*The Court has determined that the following is **not** a fundamental right:*

The right to assisted suicide. In ***Washington v. Glucksberg***, 521 U.S. 702 (1997), the Court upheld a Washington state law criminalizing assisted suicide against a challenge by physicians and gravely ill patients. The Court noted the long history of criminalizing assisted suicide in support of its ruling that the right to do so was not "deeply rooted in our nation's history and tradition."

Without expressly calling it "fundamental," the Court now TREATS as fundamental the following right:

The right to engage in same-gender sex. Until June 2003, the Supreme Court recognized no constitutional violation in the enforcement of state sodomy laws to criminalize same-gender sex. In ***Bowers v. Hardwick***, 478 U.S. 186 (1986), the Court held that there is no fundamental right to engage in homosexual sodomy, and it upheld Georgia's prosecution of a homosexual couple under the state's sodomy law. Seventeen years later, the Court overruled ***Bowers*** and held that the right to engage in homosexual sodomy in the privacy of one's home ***is*** protected under substantive due process. ***Lawrence v. Texas***, 539 U.S. 558 (2003). In so holding, the Court struck down a Texas sodomy statute that made it a crime for two persons of the same gender to engage in intimate sexual contact. Unfortunately, the majority opinion by Justice Kennedy is vague. He does not expressly state that the right to engage in same-gender sex is a ***fundamental*** right under substantive due process. Nor does he specify that statutes like the Texas sodomy law should be subject to ***strict*** scrutiny. In fact, he seems to suggest that this statute fails to satisfy rational basis review (observing, *id.* at 578, that it "furthers no legitimate state interest"). Nevertheless, he leaves no doubt that state sodomy laws directed at same-gender sex are now flatly unconstitutional. Thus, we know what the OUTCOME in these cases will be.

Watch Out!

On the Bar Exam, do ***not*** refer to same-gender sex as a "fundamental" right and do ***not*** select a Multistate answer that describes same-gender sex as a "fundamental" right. Likewise, when taking the Bar Exam, do ***not*** analyze restrictions on same-gender sex under strict scrutiny. Instead, apply rational basis review — taking care to add, if given the opportunity, that the Court has struck down such restrictions even while purporting to apply the rational basis test.

b) Scrutinizing Governmental Intrusions on Fundamental Rights — The Special Case of Abortion Rights

Any governmental action that infringes on fundamental rights is subject to strict scrutiny. This scrutiny is not always fatal — the Court still weighs the right against the state's interest in infringing on that right. The Court has upheld some restrictions on the exercise of fundamental rights, most notably upholding restrictions on the right to terminate one's pregnancy.

Although the Court established a fundamental right to terminate a pregnancy in ***Roe v. Wade***, the Court also recognized a significant state interest in protecting the fetus. The Court balanced the state interest against the right and weighed the right differently depending on the stage of pregnancy. Pursuant to the Court's "trimester" approach, in the first trimester, the woman's interest in obtaining an abortion is paramount and cannot be restricted by the state; in the second trimester, the state can impose reasonable regulations to protect the health of the mother; and in the third trimester, the state's interest is paramount — it may regulate, even proscribe, abortion, except where it is medically necessary to preserve the life or health of the mother.

In ***Planned Parenthood of Southeastern Pennsylvania v. Casey***, 505 U.S. 833 (1992), the Court rejected the ***Roe*** trimester framework because it did not adequately take into account the state's interest in protecting potential life.

A state may regulate or restrict abortion, the Court held, as long as it does not place an "undue burden" on a woman's right to obtain the abortion of a non-viable fetus. An undue burden exists if the purpose or effect of a provision of law "is to place a substantial obstacle in the path of a woman seeking an abortion before the fetus attains viability."

State measures designed to convince a woman to choose childbirth over abortion do not create an undue burden, and the state may enact regulations designed to preserve the health or life of a woman seeking an abortion as long as they do not create an undue burden. Finally, the ***Casey*** Court reaffirmed the ***Roe*** Court's holding that a state may prohibit the abortion of a viable fetus except where the abortion is necessary to protect the health or life of the mother.

Applying the "reasonable regulation" approach of ***Roe*** and the "undue burden" approach of ***Casey***, the Court has issued distinct rulings on the following types of abortion regulations:

1. **Government refusals to fund abortions**. The Court has held that in structuring welfare programs, the government may constitutionally choose not to fund abortions. Thus, in ***Maher v. Roe***, 432 U.S. 464 (1977), the Court upheld a Connecticut law granting Medicaid benefits for childbirth but denying them for non-therapeutic, medically unnecessary abortions.

Similarly, in ***Harris v. McRae***, 448 U.S. 297 (1980), the Court rejected constitutional challenges to federal funding limitations that barred payments even for most medically necessary abortions.

2. **Government refusals to fund family planning counseling that includes abortion as an option.** The Supreme Court has upheld a regulation forbidding any recipient of federal family planning funds from mentioning abortion as a family planning option when counseling patients. ***Rust v. Sullivan***, 500 U.S. 173 (1991).

3. **Spousal consent and notice requirements.** The Court has struck down laws requiring women seeking abortions to demonstrate that they have secured spousal consent or communicated spousal notification. ***Planned Parenthood of Central Missouri v. Danforth***, 428 U.S. 52 (1976) (invalidating spousal consent requirement); ***Planned Parenthood of Southeastern Pennsylvania v. Casey***, 505 U.S. 833 (1992) (invalidating spousal notification requirement).

4. **Parental consent and notice requirements.** The Court has repeatedly upheld state laws that require parental consent as long as those laws contain some provision for judicial bypass of such a requirement. In addition, the Court sustained a state law requiring a physician to notify parents of a minor who obtains an abortion, and has upheld laws requiring notification of one or both parents when a judicial bypass procedure was available.

   When a law places obstacles in the path of teenagers seeking abortions (obstacles, for example, like a parental-notice requirement or a waiting period), a medical-emergency exception is constitutionally required. In other words, any such statute must contain an exception to the parental-notice or waiting-period requirement that is triggered if, in appropriate medical judgment, the teenager is facing a medical emergency that threatens her life or health. ***Ayotte v. Planned Parenthood of Northern New England,*** 546 U.S. 320 (2006).

5. **Requiring all second-trimester abortions to be performed in a hospital.** Calling it a "significant obstacle in the path of a woman seeking an abortion," the Supreme Court struck down a state law that required all second-trimester abortions to be performed in a hospital. ***City of Akron v. Akron Center for Reproductive Health***, 462 U.S. 416 (1983).

6. **State-mandated "informed consent" counseling designed to persuade a woman to choose childbirth over abortion.** In ***Planned Parenthood of Southeastern Pennsylvania v. Casey***, 505 U.S. 833 (1992), the Supreme Court upheld a variety of State-mandated "informed consent" procedures — requiring that a physician must apprise the woman "of the probable

gestational age of the unborn child" and make her aware of printed materials published by the State that describe the fetus and offer information about medical assistance for childbirth, child support from the father, adoption agencies, and other services affording an alternative to abortion. In concluding that these requirements did not offend the "undue burden" test, the Court asserted that it is permissible for a State "to further its legitimate goal of protecting the life of the unborn by enacting legislation aimed at ensuring a decision that is mature and informed, even when in so doing the State expresses a preference for childbirth over abortion." 505 U.S. at 883.

7. **State-mandated 24-hour waiting period.** The ***Casey*** decision also upheld a requirement that the abortion not be performed until at least 24 hours after the woman has received the "informed consent" counseling. The Court held that this 24-hour waiting period did not offend the undue burden test, even though the record contained "troubling" evidence that it would create a substantial hardship for many women. 505 U.S. at 886.

8. **Prohibiting "partial-birth" abortions.** After striking down a nearly identical ban in 2000, the Supreme Court (animated by a new conservative majority) abruptly reversed course, upholding the federal Partial-Birth Abortion Ban Act by a 5-to-4 vote. ***Gonzales v. Carhart***, 127 S. Ct. 1610 (2007). This is the first time that the Court has ever upheld a prohibition on a particular method of abortion. The statute subjects doctors to fines and prison terms for performing one variation (the so-called "intact" D & E method) of a common second-trimester abortion procedure. In another departure from its abortion precedents, the Court ruled that the statute's failure to include a health-of-the-mother exception did **not** make it unconstitutional. 127 S. Ct. at 1635-38.

Watch Out!

Though it purports to reaffirm ***Casey's*** "undue burden" test, ***Gonzales v. Carhart*** may inaugurate a new and far more deferential treatment of abortion restrictions by the Supreme Court. Writing for the four dissenters, Justice Ginsburg called the decision "alarming," said that it "blurs the line ... between previability and postviability abortions," and stressed: "[F]or the first time since ***Roe***, the Court blesses a prohibition with no exception safeguarding a woman's health." 127 S. Ct. at 1641 (Ginsburg, J., dissenting).

c) Non-Fundamental Rights

Government intrusions on non-fundamental rights are subject to minimal scrutiny. The Court applies rational basis review and will uphold governmental intrusions on non-fundamental rights as long as they are **rationally related to a legitimate government purpose**. In practice, this level of review is toothless — the Court almost never finds a violation of substantive due process when the government's actions infringe on non-fundamental rights.

1. **Property and Economic Rights**
   In ***Lochner v. New York***, 198 U.S. 45 (1905), the Supreme Court held that freedom of contract is a fundamental right embodied in the "liberty" protected by the Due Process Clause of the Fourteenth Amendment. The Court struck down a New York state law that limited the working hours of bakers because it violated the freedom of contract of the workers. Following ***Lochner***, the Court repeatedly struck down both state and federal legislation protecting workers and consumers on the grounds that the legislation violated that freedom of contract. However, the Court's approach came under increasing attack as being overly intrusive to the legislative process and embodying the justices' personal beliefs rather than constitutional doctrine.

   In ***West Coast Hotel v. Parrish***, 300 U.S. 379 (1937), the Court rejected its reasoning in ***Lochner***, stating that "the Constitution does not recognize an absolute and uncontrollable liberty." Since that ruling, the Court has virtually abandoned substantive due process in the economic realm, taking an approach toward economic regulation that is extremely deferential to legislatures. The Court applies minimal scrutiny to both the ends and means of economic-based legislation, and "the law need not be in every respect logically consistent with its aims to be constitutional. It is enough that there be an evil at hand for correction, and that it might be thought that the particular legislative measure was a rational way to correct it." ***Williamson v. Lee Optical Co.***, 348 U.S. 482 (1955).

d) Retroactive Legislation
Retroactive legislation may be unconstitutional on the grounds that it violates substantive due process. For example, in the case of ***Eastern Enterprises v. Apfel***, 524 U.S. 498 (1998), the Court considered the constitutionality of provisions of the Coal Industry Retiree Health Benefits Act of 1992 that required companies that had previously employed coal miners to bear a certain portion of the miners' health care costs in retirement. Four justices found the provision to be a regulatory taking subject to the Just Compensation Clause of the Fifth Amendment. But in a concurrence, Justice Kennedy stated that he would find the law to be an unconstitutional violation of the substantive due process rights of the plaintiff coal company. Because the statute created liability for events which occurred 35 years ago, Justice Kennedy argued that "the case before us represents one of the rare instances where the Legislature has exceeded the limits imposed by due process." Justice Kennedy's concurrence indicates that the Court might be willing to

revive the doctrine of substantive due process in the economic realm, at least to the extent of striking down retroactive legislation.

c. Takings

The Takings Clause of the Fifth Amendment provides "nor shall private property be taken for public use, without just compensation." Both the federal government and the states have the power of **eminent domain** — the Takings Clause places a limit on that power, and has been interpreted to limit both the state and federal governments. The process for determining whether there has been a taking, and how much compensation is constitutionally required, is similar to that triggered by the Due Process Clause. However, courts are more likely to find that a taking has occurred, and are more generous in ordering compensation, than they are in the realm of procedural due process.

Analysis under the Takings Clause can be divided into **four questions: First, is there a taking? Second, is it "property"? Third, if there is a taking of property, the next question is whether it was for public use? And fourth, has just compensation been paid?** The four steps are addressed separately below:

1) Is There a Taking?

There are two types of takings — possessory takings and regulatory takings. A possessory taking occurs when the government physically confiscates or occupies property. A regulatory taking occurs when a government regulation deprives the owner of an economically viable use of his property or limits that use. Most of the litigation regarding the Takings Clause focuses on the threshold question of whether there is a taking to begin with.

a) Possessory takings

The Court generally finds a taking when the government has physically occupied or confiscated property. The confiscation of property is the most classic case of a possessory taking. For example, in ***Webb Fabulous Pharmacies, Inc. v. Beckwith***, 449 U.S. 155 (1980), the Court found a taking when the government took the interest accruing in an interpleader account, because it amounted to government expropriation of private property. The occupation of property can occur in various manners. For example, in ***Pumpelly v. Green Bay Co.,*** 80 U.S. 166 (1878), the Court found a taking when the building of a dam resulted in the flooding of the property owner's basement. The Court will find a taking even if the occupation is of a very small area. In ***Loretto v. Teleprompter Manhattan CATV Corp.***, 458 U.S. 419 (1982), the Court found a taking when a city ordinance required the owners of apartment buildings to make space available for television cables. Similarly, the presence of a telephone line, underground pipes or wires, or rails would amount to a taking because of the physical space that they occupy, no matter how small or unobtrusive.

The Court is less consistent when determining whether access to property amounts to a physical occupation. In making this determination, the Court will weigh "such factors as the character of the government action, its economic impact, and its interference with reasonable investment-backed expectations." ***PruneYard Shopping Center v. Robins***, 447 U.S. 74 (1980). These criteria are so general that they give the courts a lot of discretion and latitude. For example, in ***Kaiser Aetna v. United States***, 444 U.S. 164 (1979), the Court found a physical occupation when the government required that a waterway be opened for public use. By contrast, in ***Pruneyard***, the Court found that a California court requiring a privately owned shopping mall to open itself up to speech activities did not amount to a physical occupation, so there was no taking.

The Court is also somewhat inconsistent in whether or not government occupation or possession might not be a taking in an emergency situation. In ***United States v. Caltex, Inc.***, 344 U.S. 149 (1952), the Court held that there was not a taking when the government destroyed a company's oil fields in the Phillipines to keep them from being taken over by the Japanese during World War II. More recently, however, the Court has indicated that there is no emergency exception to the requirement of just compensation for takings. In ***Lucas v. South Carolina Coastal Council***, 505 U.S. 1003 (1992), the Court said, "In general [at least with regard to permanent invasions], no matter how minute the intrusion, and no matter how weighty the public purpose behind it, we have required compensation."

b) Regulatory Takings

In the landmark case of ***Pennsylvania Coal v. Mahon***, 260 U.S. 393 (1922), the Court stated that government regulation of property could be considered to be a taking if it went "too far." In that case, the Court found a taking when government regulation barred the mining of coal in any manner that would cause the subsidence of property, because that regulation prevented the company from exercising certain mining rights. **The current Supreme Court is extremely receptive to finding government regulations to be takings, including environmental regulations,** and this is an area where the current Court has been quite active in its rulings.

Government regulation of private property is a taking whenever the regulation permanently deprives the owner of all economically viable uses of his land. ***Lucas v. South Carolina Coastal Council***, 505 U.S. 1003 (1992). But ***temporary*** bans, halting development while government officials formulate a land-use plan, are ***not*** a per se taking; so long as they are reasonable, such delays do not constitute a regulatory taking. ***Tahoe-Sierra Preservation Council, Inc. v. Tahoe Regional Planning Agency***, 535 U.S. 302 (2002) (holding that 32-month moratorium on development during environmental study for comprehensive land-use plan did not constitute a regulatory taking).

In ***Lucas***, for example, the Court found a taking when a South Carolina law prohibiting beachfront development in areas likely to be affected by hurricanes prohibited the property owner from building real estate on his beachfront land. In contrast, in ***Penn Central Transportation Co. v. City of New York***, 438 U.S. 104 (1978), the Court found no taking when a government designation of Penn Station as a historical landmark prohibited development on top of the station, because the regulation did not deprive the owners of all profitable use of the building.

The Court is more reluctant to find zoning ordinances to be regulatory takings. For example, in ***Goldblatt v. Town of Hempstead***, 369 U.S. 590 (1962), the Court found no taking when a city zoning ordinance prevented further excavation of a stone and gravel quarry that had been in operation for years. Recently, however, the Court has indicated that it is more receptive to takings challenges to zoning ordinances if they limit the reasonable expectations of owners to develop their property as they desired. For example, in ***Dolan v. City of Tigard***, 512 U.S. 374 (1994), the Court found a regulatory taking when a local zoning ordinance conditioned the permit to expand a building on the owner's willingness to allow an easement for a bike path to run through his property.

In ***Dolan***, the Court established a two-part test for determining whether a government regulation that imposes a condition on the development of property is a regulatory taking. **First, it must be shown that the condition is rationally related to the government's purpose for regulating. Second, it must be shown that the burden created by the regulation is roughly proportionate to the government's reason for regulating.** The Court indicated that in applying this test, it would weigh the property owner's interest heavily and view the government's purpose skeptically, and it is likely that the Court will continue to find regulatory takings in this type of case.

Finally, one who purchases property after restrictions on development are already in place may still challenge those restrictions as a taking. ***Palazzolo v. Rhode Island***, 533 U.S. 606 (2001).

2) Is It "Property"?
As in the area of procedural due process, the Court generally relies on non-constitutional sources, such as state law, to determine whether there is a property interest. Property is defined by the reasonable expectations of the owner based on the positive law at the time that the property was purchased. For example, in ***Lucas***, the Court said that whether there was a taking depended on whether a coastal preservation act was in effect, limiting development of beachfront property, at the time the developer purchased the beachfront property.

3) Was the Taking for "Public Use"?
If the property was not taken for public use, the government must give it back.

However, the Court defines public use very broadly and applies a deferential test for determining whether the property was taken for public use. The Court has said that a taking is for public use so long as it is "rationally related to a conceivably public purpose." ***Hawaii Housing Authority v. Midkiff***, 465 U.S. 1097 (1984). Therefore, it is highly unlikely that a claim for a taking would not satisfy this step.

More recently, the Court held that the "public use" requirement was even satisfied where the government used its eminent domain powers to take property in furtherance of an economic development plan — where, in essence, the government was confiscating property from one private owner and giving it to another private owner. ***Kelo v. City of New London***, 545 U.S. 469 (2005).

4) Has Just Compensation Been Paid?
In determining whether just compensation has been paid, just compensation is measured in terms of loss to the owner, rather than gain to the government. For example, in ***Lucas***, the owner of the beachfront property recovered $1.2 million from the state because that would have been the market value of the land had he been allowed to develop it.

d. Incorporation of Bill of Rights
The First Ten Amendments to the Constitution, known as the Bill of Rights, are enforceable only against the federal government, and were interpreted not to limit state governments in the case of ***Barron v. Baltimore***, 32 U.S. 243 (1833).

But after the Civil War, the Fourteenth Amendment was adopted with the specific aim of restricting the power of state and local governments to infringe the fundamental rights of the American people. Within the Fourteenth Amendment, the Due Process Clause specifically bars state and local governments from depriving life, liberty, or property without due process of law. The liberty guarantee in the Due Process Clause has come to be viewed by the Court as a **funnel** or **passageway** through which the key provisions of the Bill of Rights may be applied to state and local governments. Thus, in 1925 the Court held that the First Amendment freedom of speech applies to the states via the Fourteenth Amendment's Due Process Clause. ***Gitlow v. New York,*** 268 U.S. 652, 666 (1925).

In the middle of the twentieth century, the justices of the Supreme Court engaged in a lively debate over whether the framers of the Fourteenth Amendment intended the Due Process Clause to incorporate all of the rights in the Bill of Rights, or whether they intended those rights to be incorporated selectively. In ***Palko v. Connecticut***, 302 U.S. 319 (1937), the Court adopted the **"selective incorporation" approach,** holding that the **Due Process Clause only incorporated "fundamental rights"** that were "implicit in the concept of ordered liberty."

The Court has never abandoned its selective approach to incorporation. However, during the years of the Warren Court, the Court found almost every right guaranteed by the Bill of Rights to be "fundamental" and incorporated them against the states in a series of cases mostly involving the rights of criminal defendants. For example, in ***Duncan v. Louisiana***, 391 U.S. 145 (1968), the Court held the Sixth Amendment right to trial by jury to be fundamental, striking down a Louisiana law that only provided a jury trial for criminal defendants risking capital punishment or hard labor.

However, the question remains whether the incorporation of the right against the state implicates all of the Court's jurisprudence regarding that right in the federal context. For example, does the right to trial by jury include the right to a jury of 12 members, guaranteed in federal trials? In ***Williams v. Florida,*** 399 U.S. 78 (1970), the Court held that the 12-member panel is not a "necessary ingredient" of the Sixth Amendment right to trial by jury. However, uncertainty remains as to what is a "necessary ingredient" of federal rights incorporated against the states in other contexts.

e. The Contracts Clause

Article I, §10 provides that "No state shall . . . pass any . . . law impairing the obligation of Contracts."

> **Watch Out!**
>
> The Contracts Clause is **not** a *source* of federal legislative power, but is rather a *restriction* on the exercise of *state* legislative power.
>
> This provision applies only if a state or local law interferes with **existing** contracts, not government regulation of future contracts. Moreover, the Contracts Clause does ***not*** apply to the federal government – challenges to federal interference with contracts must be brought pursuant to the Due Process Clause.

The Contracts Clause has been interpreted to be extremely limited in scope. The state has broad powers to interfere with contracts in emergency situations. For example, in ***Home Building & Loan Association v. Blaisdell***, 290 U.S. 398 (1934), the Court upheld a Minnesota law that prohibited lenders from foreclosing on mortgages from 1933 until May 1, 1935. The Court upheld the law because it was an emergency measure designed to alleviate the impact of the Great Depression and to "protect the vital interests of the community."

In determining whether a state law violates the Contracts Clause, the Court applies a three-part test. First, is there a substantial impairment of a contractual relationship? Second, if so, does it serve a significant and legitimate public purpose? Third, is it rationally related to achieving that goal? This test, which is similar to rational basis review of economic legislation, is extremely deferential to the state and very rarely results in the finding of a constitutional violation.

In fact, since 1934, the Court has only once found a state law to violate the Contracts Clause. In that case, ***Allied Structural Steel Co. v. Spannaus***, 438 U.S. 234 (1978), the Court struck down a Minnesota law which required employers to pay a pension funding charge if they terminated a pension plan or closed a Minnesota office. But in the intervening years since 1978, the Court has not followed ***Allied Structural***, so it is difficult to tell whether the case is an anomaly or one that might someday be used to revitalize the Contracts Clause.

MBE Advice

At present time, the Contracts Clause seems to be a dead letter — and when it appears on the Multistate Bar Exam, it is almost always a red herring.

f. Equal Protection

Note: Before delving into the Equal Protection Clause, here are some materials that you should MEMORIZE in preparation for the Bar Exam:

1) There are three tests that govern equal protection claims: **strict** scrutiny, **intermediate** scrutiny, and **rational basis** review.
   a) Under strict scrutiny, the challenged regulation must be **necessary** to achieve a **compelling** governmental purpose.
   b) Under intermediate scrutiny, the regulation must be **substantially** related to an **important** governmental purpose.
   c) Under rational basis review, the regulation need only be **rationally** related to a **legitimate** governmental purpose.

2) The baseline, presumptive standard is **rational basis** review. (It governs, for example, any **economic** regulation.)

3) **Heightened** scrutiny applies when the government creates discriminatory classifications that affect **either**...
   a) a **fundamental right**, or
   b) a **suspect class**.

4) For equal protection purposes, the following are **fundamental rights** — which are governed by **strict scrutiny**:
   a) The right to **vote**.
   b) The right to **travel** (but see ***Saenz v. Roe***, 526 U.S. 489, 502-03 (1999), which found a textual home for the right to travel in the long-ignored Privileges or Immunities Clause of the 14th Amendment).

c) The right to **privacy** (e.g., ***Skinner v. Oklahoma***, 316 U.S. 535 (1942), which struck down a sterilization-of-criminals law).

5) As for suspect, semi-suspect, and non-suspect **classifications**, be sure to memorize each of the following classifications with its corresponding level of scrutiny:
   a) **Race** (including affirmative action) — **strict** scrutiny.
   b) **National origin** — **strict** scrutiny.
   c) **Alienage** (i.e., non-citizens) — **strict** scrutiny.
   d) **Gender** — **intermediate** scrutiny.
   e) **Non-marital children** — **intermediate** scrutiny.
   f) **Wealth** — **rational basis** review.
   g) **Age** — **rational basis** review.
   h) **Mental disability** — **rational basis** review.
   i) **Sexual orientation** — **rational basis** review.

The Equal Protection Clause of the Fourteenth Amendment provides that **"no state shall make or enforce any law which shall . . . deny to any person within its jurisdiction the equal protection of the laws."** Originally intended to protect newly freed slaves following the Civil War, the Clause has been found to protect all people from unequal treatment by the state.

Watch Out!

Although the Fourteenth Amendment only limits **state and local** governments, the Court has also applied equal protection doctrine to the **federal** government by reading the doctrine into the Due Process Clause of the Fifth Amendment.

1) **General**
   The essential principle behind the Equal Protection Clause is that people who are similarly situated must be treated equally. Courts apply varying levels of scrutiny to state laws and policies depending on the nature of the interest at stake, and whether or not the person challenging the state action belongs to a suspect class. **Equal protection challenges are triggered when a state creates a classification that differentiates between people.** At minimum, equal protection requires that a legislative classification be reasonable, and that it have a fair and substantial relation to the object of the legislation.

   The baseline for equal protection analysis is **rational basis review**. Rational basis review applies if no fundamental interest or suspect class is affected by the challenged action. **If the classification affects a fundamental right or a suspect class, reviewing courts apply a heightened level of review.**

a) **Discriminatory Purpose and Effect**
The Court has held that the Equal Protection Clause only prohibits **intentional** discrimination. If a government policy or practice unintentionally has a disparate impact on a protected class, that impact is not sufficient to violate equal protection. In addition, **discriminatory motive alone is not enough — there must also be some discriminatory effect. However, the policy or practice need not discriminate on its face to violate equal protection — a facially neutral law may be found to be purposefully discriminatory because of its discriminatory application.**

Discriminatory impact, absent discriminatory intent, is insufficient to establish a cause of action for violation of equal protection. For example, in ***Washington v. Davis***, 426 U.S. 229 (1976), African-American applicants for positions as District of Columbia police officers challenged the validity of a qualifying test administered to candidates for the job. They argued that the test violated equal protection because a higher percentage of blacks than whites failed the test and the test had not been validated for its ability to measure subsequent job performance. The Court rejected the claim, stating that the discriminatory impact of the test alone did not violate equal protection.

Discriminatory motive alone is not enough to violate equal protection. There must also be a showing of discriminatory effect. For example, in the case of ***Palmer v. Thompson***, 403 U.S. 217 (1971), the Court held that the city of Jackson, Mississippi had not acted unconstitutionally in closing its public pools even though there was some evidence that city officials closed the pools to avoid integrating them. The Court noted that there was also substantial evidence that the city thought integrated pools could not be operated safely and economically, and found no discriminatory effect because the city had no affirmative duty to operate swimming pools. Stating, "no case in this Court has held that a legislative act may violate equal protection solely because of the motivations of the men who voted for it," the Court upheld the closing of the pools.

However, **a policy or practice need not discriminate on its face to be found purposefully discriminatory if its administration indicates the intent to discriminate.** For example, in ***Yick Wo v. Hopkins***, 118 U.S. 356 (1886), the Court struck down a San Francisco ordinance that prohibited operating a laundry in a wood building without a permit. Though the law was facially neutral, the Court found that in practice the city of San Francisco had denied permits to all Chinese applicants, but granted them to almost all white applicants. The Court stated, "Though the law itself be fair on its face and impartial in appearance, yet, if it is applied and administered with an evil eye and an unequal hand . . . the denial of equal justice is still within the prohibition of the Constitution."

The ruling in ***Yick Wo*** means that plaintiffs can use statistical information to establish purposeful discrimination. For example, in cases regarding voting rights and employment, the Court has held that purposeful discrimination may be inferred from statistical data. Bear in mind that if the statistics only show a disproportionate impact, they will be insufficient to establish a violation of equal protection. ***Yick Wo*** simply means that **statistics can be used as evidence to prove intentional discrimination.**

2) Economic Regulation — Rational Basis Review

Economic regulations are subject to the most minimal level of scrutiny — rational basis review. Under rational basis review, a court will uphold a classification as long as it is rationally related to a legitimate state purpose. This level of review is extremely deferential to the legislature, and challenges based on rational basis review are very rarely successful.

For example, the Court upheld an Oklahoma state law that prohibited any person not a licensed optometrist or ophthalmologist from fitting eyeglass lenses without a prescription from a licensed optometrist or ophthalmologist. The law was challenged by opticians, and subjected to rational basis review. The Court upheld the statute, stating, "It is enough that there is an evil at hand for correction, and that it might be thought that the particular legislative measure was a rational way to correct it." ***Williamson v. Lee Optical***, 348 U.S. 483 (1955).

This minimal level of scrutiny extends to classifications that differentiate on the basis of personal wealth. In ***Dandridge v. Williams***, 397 U.S. 417 (1970), the Court declined to find poverty to be a suspect class and held that there is no fundamental right to subsistence benefits. Because no suspect class or fundamental right was at stake, the Court treated a Maryland law setting family caps on welfare benefits as an economic regulation. The Court applied rational basis review and upheld the law.

3) Fundamental Rights — Strict Scrutiny

Construing the Equal Protection Clause, the Court has held **the right to vote, the right to travel,** and **the right to privacy** to be fundamental rights that trigger **strict scrutiny** of government actions that infringe on those rights. **Strict scrutiny, the highest level of review, requires that a governmental classification be necessary to achieve a compelling governmental interest.** Strict scrutiny is almost always "fatal in fact." Government action rarely survives this test.

a) The Right to Vote

Although a state is not required to allow people to vote for any particular political office, and the right to vote itself is not guaranteed by the Constitution, "once the franchise is granted, lines may not be drawn that are inconsistent with the Equal Protection Clause." ***Harper v. Virginia Board of Elections***, 383 U.S. 663 (1966). The Court has held the right to vote to be a fundamental right, and has struck down a number of restrictions on that right. Notably, although the Court does not recognize poverty to be a protected class, the Court has struck down a number of wealth-based classifications that restricted the right to vote and run for political office.

1. **One person, one vote**
   In ***Reynolds v. Sims***, 377 U.S. 533 (1964), the Court held that equal protection requires that districts for electing state legislatures must be apportioned so as to satisfy the rule of "one person, one vote." The Court stated, "an individual's right to vote for state legislators is unconstitutionally impaired when its weight is in substantial fashion diluted when compared to the voices of citizens living in other parts of the state." As a result, representation in a state legislature must be evenly proportioned unless the legislature has a legitimate state objective that demands otherwise.

2. **Poll taxes and property qualifications**
   The Twenty-Fourth Amendment forbids conditioning the right to vote in a federal election on payment of a poll tax, but it does not apply to state elections. In ***Harper v. Virginia Board of Elections***, 383 U.S. 663 (1966), however, the Court declared the imposition of a poll tax by the state of Virginia to be a violation of equal protection. The Court applied strict scrutiny, but indicated that the poll tax was not even rationally based, stating, "Voter qualifications have no relation to wealth, nor to paying or not paying this or any other tax." Applying similar reasoning, the Court struck down a Louisiana law that restricted the vote to property owners in ***Cipriano v. Houma***, 395 U.S. 701 (1969) (per curiam).

3. **Photo ID Requirements**
   A voter identification law, which requires would-be voters to present current state or federal photo identification as a prerequisite to casting a ballot, does not violate the right to vote under the Equal Protection Clause. ***Crawford v. Marion County Election Board***, 128 S. Ct. 1610 (2008). *The Court did NOT apply strict scrutiny here* — but it reaffirmed the applicability of strict scrutiny when analyzing poll taxes, and it suggested that heightened scrutiny should be applied to any restriction that conditions the right to vote upon a status or characteristic (like wealth) that is unrelated to a voter's true qualifications. In the Court's view, a photo ID requirement is distinguishable from a poll tax because it helps to combat voter fraud and is therefore properly focused upon voter qualifications and electoral integrity.

   Instead of applying strict scrutiny, the Court reaffirmed its commitment to a balancing test when analyzing "'evenhanded restrictions that protect the integrity and reliability of the electoral process itself.'" 128 S. Ct. at 1616 (quoting ***Anderson v. Celebrezze***, 460 U.S. 780, 788 n.9 (1983)). *Under that balancing test, a state law's burden on a political party, an individual* *voter, or a discrete class of voters must be justified by relevant and legitimate state interests sufficiently weighty to justify the restriction.* 128 S. Ct. at 1616. Applying that balancing test, the Court acknowledged that any photo ID requirement will impose some hardship upon poor and elderly voters, but it stressed that the governmental interest in preventing voter fraud was sufficiently weighty to justify the restriction.

4. **Ballot access**

While prohibiting poll taxes and property qualifications for votes protects the right to vote, the Court also applies heightened scrutiny to protect the rights of candidates to gain access to the ballot. For example, in ***Bullock v. Carter***, 405 U.S. 134 (1972), the Court struck down a Texas system that required candidates to finance the cost of local elections by paying filing fees of thousands of dollars. The Court noted, "We would ignore reality were we not to recognize that this system falls with unequal weight on voters, as well as candidates, according to their economic status."

Equal protection principles do not absolutely prohibit the payment of filing fees by candidates, however. In ***Lubin v. Parish***, 415 U.S. 709 (1974), the Court upheld a California law requiring the payment of filing fees of over $700 to run in a local election, requiring only that the state waive the filing fee for candidates who could show that they were indigent.

b) **The Right to Travel**

The "right to travel" is also a fundamental right, and government interference with that right triggers strict scrutiny. [For an explication of the right to travel, ***see supra*** § I (E)(3) of this outline, discussing the Privileges and Immunities of National Citizenship.] In ***Shapiro v. Thompson***, 394 U.S. 618 (1969), the Court held unconstitutional federal and state welfare provisions that denied welfare benefits to new residents of a state who had resided there for less than one year. The Court held that the denial of benefits impermissibly interfered with the constitutional guarantee that "all citizens be free to travel throughout the length and breadth of our land." Relying on similar reasoning, in ***Memorial Hospital v. Maricopa County***, 415 U.S. 250 (1974), the Court struck down a state statute requiring a year's residence in a county before an indigent could receive county-subsidized non-emergency medical care.

In ***Shapiro*** and ***Maricopa***, the Court applied equal protection analysis because it saw the states as differentiating between two classes of people — new residents and long-time residents. More recently, however, the Court has clarified that the right to travel is located not in the Equal Protection Clause but in the Privileges or Immunities Clause of the Fourteenth Amendment. ***Saenz v. Roe***, 526 U.S. 489 (1999). In ***Saenz***, the Court indicated that the right to travel is so fundamental that no state purpose could be sufficient to justify welfare regulations that granted lower levels of benefits to newly-arrived residents than those available to long-time residents of the state. If you are confronted with a right-to-travel issue, apply **strict scrutiny,** 526 U.S. at 504.

c) The Right to Privacy

Although the right to privacy is generally linked to substantive due process protections, the fundamental nature of privacy rights also triggers equal protection because of the danger that the government will interfere with those rights based on prejudice against powerless minorities. For example, in the case of ***Skinner v. Oklahoma***, 316 U.S. 535 (1942), the Court relied on equal protection principles in striking down a state law that allowed for the sterilization of persons twice convicted of crimes of moral turpitude. Recognizing procreation as "fundamental to the very existence and survival of the race," the Court was concerned that the classification had been promulgated against a relatively powerless minority — that of poor (as opposed to white collar) criminals. Pursuant to the ***Skinner*** case, a reviewing court will apply strict scrutiny to government classifications based on reproduction and, by implication, other recognized privacy rights.

d) The Right of Access to the Courts

In a series of cases involving access to the courts, the Court has held that access to some adjudicative processes may not be denied solely on the basis of inability to pay filing fees. As is the case with voting, there is no constitutional right to litigate cases and states may decide to replace many adjudicative processes with alternative dispute resolution or other decision-making measures. But once the state has granted a right to a process, it cannot be denied solely on the basis of inability to pay. For example, in ***Griffin v. Illinois***, 351 U.S. 12 (1956), the Court held that once the state of Illinois had created an appeal **as of right** for criminal defendants, it could not do so "in a way that discriminates against some convicted defendants on account of their poverty." In ***Griffin***, the Court held that an indigent criminal defendant had a right to waiver of the cost of preparing a trial transcript in connection with an appeal as of right. However, a state need not provide counsel for criminal defendants attempting to invoke **discretionary** review. ***Ross v. Moffitt***, 417 U.S. 600 (1974).

The Court applies a hybrid approach to these cases, combining principles of due process and equal protection to create a right of access to the courts for indigent persons in some adjudicative processes. In determining which adjudicative processes trigger these rights, the Court focuses not only on the extent to which those processes are discretionary, but also the extent to which they involve fundamental interests on the part of the litigants. In ***Griffin***, for example, the defendant had a fundamental interest in overturning his criminal conviction to get out of jail. In ***Boddie v. Connecticut***, 401 U.S. 371 (1971), the Court recognized a right to petition for waiver of filing fees for divorce because of the fundamental nature of the family interests at stake.

More recently, in the case of ***MLB v. SLJ***, 519 U.S. 102 (1996), the Court found a right to petition for waiver of fees associated with the appeal of the termination of parental rights because of the fundamental nature of those rights. In contrast, the Court found no right to waiver of filing fees in a bankruptcy case because purely economic interests were at stake. ***United States v. Kras***, 409 U.S. 434 (1973).

4) Other Rights

Since the early 1970s, the Court has been reluctant to find any more fundamental rights in its equal protection jurisprudence. Most notably, the Court has refused to find a fundamental right to welfare benefits and education. But even while purporting to apply rational basis review, the Court has **tacitly** applied heightened scrutiny to strike down government policies infringing on the receipt of government benefits and public education in some cases.

a) No Right to Welfare Benefits

In ***Dandridge v. Williams***, 397 U.S. 417 (1970), the Court ruled that there is no constitutional right to welfare benefits. However, in the case of ***Department of Agriculture v. Moreno***, 413 U.S. 528 (1973), the Court noted that those benefits cannot be denied based on mere prejudice. In ***Moreno***, the Court struck down a food stamp regulation denying stamps to households containing unrelated members. The Court found that Congress had been motivated by prejudice against hippies in enacting the law; thus there was no rational basis to support it. Though the ***Moreno*** Court purported to apply rational basis review, it seems tacitly to have employed heightened scrutiny, and the opinion is generally viewed as an anomaly.

b) The Right to Education

The Court has taken inconsistent positions on whether there is a fundamental right to education. In ***San Antonio Independent School District v. Rodriguez***, 411 U.S. 1 (1973), the Court stated that there is no fundamental right to education. But nine years later, the Court barred the state of Texas from expelling all children of illegal immigrants from its public schools. In ***Plyler v. Doe***, 457 U.S. 202 (1982), the Court ruled that the state of Texas could not constitutionally deny public education to children of illegal immigrants. Neither a suspect class nor a fundamental right was at stake and the Court purported to apply rational basis review — but it tacitly applied a heightened level of scrutiny. The Court held that the law was impermissible because it would perpetuate an underclass, indicating that the tacitly heightened standard may have been based on the combination of interests at stake, as well as the innocent nature of the children who were being denied the education.

g. Suspect Classifications

The Court will also apply a heightened standard of review to governmental classifications that have an adverse impact on a suspect class. In the famous footnote

4 to ***U.S. v. Carolene Products Co.,*** 304 U.S. 144 (1938), Justice Stone indicated that heightened review would be justified when government action unfavorably affects "discrete and insular minorities" that systematically tend to lose in the political process. In later cases, the Court has added that a suspect class should also be based on an immutable characteristic, such as race or gender.

Once the Court has determined that a classification affects a suspect class, the Court applies a heightened standard of review that varies in accordance with the nature of the suspect class. **The Court has found racial and ancestral groups to merit the highest level of scrutiny, strict scrutiny. More recently, the Court has applied a lower level of heightened scrutiny, known as intermediate scrutiny, to classifications based on gender and illegitimacy. The Court has rejected arguments for heightened scrutiny for classifications based on poverty and mental disability.**

1) Race or National Origin — Strict Scrutiny

Classifications based on race or national origin are subjected to strict scrutiny, requiring the classification to be necessary to advance a compelling governmental purpose. This was first acknowledged by the Court in ***Korematsu v. United States***, 323 U.S. 214 (1944). Ironically, the ***Korematsu*** Court upheld the internment of Japanese-Americans despite its stated application of strict scrutiny. However, in more recent cases the Court has applied the standard with teeth, striking down almost every government classification based on race and national origin.

For example, in ***Palmore v. Sidoti***, 466 U.S. 429 (1984), the Court overruled a state court decision denying custody to the divorced white mother of a white child who remarried to a black man. The lower court had granted custody to the white father on the grounds that the child would inevitably suffer from social stigmatization if she remained with her mother and stepfather. The Court acknowledged that the daughter might suffer from some stigma, but found that government action was not necessary to achieving a compelling governmental purpose because the reality of private biases are not permissible considerations for removing an infant child from her mother.

a) School Desegregation

i) Rejecting the "separate but equal" doctrine

In ***Brown v. Board of Education***, 347 U.S. 483 (1954), the Court ruled unconstitutional the segregation of schools based on race, and rejected the doctrine of "separate but equal" that had prevailed since the earlier ruling of ***Plessy v. Ferguson***, 163 U.S. 537 (1896). In subsequent cases, the Court ordered segregated districts to use "all deliberate speed" to end segregation, and sanctioned the cross-town busing of students as a remedy. However, the Court drew the line at the school district border, holding that inter-district busing was not constitutionally mandated in ***Milliken v. Bradley***, 418 U.S. 717 (1974).

ii) "De jure" versus "de facto" segregation

As discussed above, a discriminatory motive is necessary for a finding of a constitutional violation in the area of school segregation, as in other areas of equal protection law. The Court has ruled that only "de jure" segregation (segregation by law) is unconstitutional, but that the Equal Protection Clause does not prohibit "de facto" discrimination that might result from neighborhood-based schools in racially-segregated neighborhoods. However, in ***Keyes v. School District***, 413 U.S. 189 (1973), a case involving the schools of Denver, the Court adopted a test to make it relatively easy to find de jure discrimination — such a finding is warranted when intentional discrimination is present in any **part** of a school district. The ***Keyes*** case opened up desegregation in northern cities since a finding of intentional discrimination in any part of a district would warrant a district-wide remedy. In later cases involving Columbus and Dayton, Ohio, the Court narrowed its ruling, noting that discriminatory intent would only be inferred when the actions and practices of the school boards had the effect of aggravating, rather than alleviating, racial segregation.

iii) Relinquishing judicial oversight of "successfully" desegregated school districts

The cases involving school desegregation, especially those mandating busing, were extremely controversial and often required federal district courts to oversee school boards for long periods of time, as much as twenty years. More recently, the issue has been when may federal courts declare the school districts to be successfully desegregated and relinquish their jurisdiction over the school boards. In ***Board of Education of Oklahoma City v. Dowell***, 498 U.S. 237 (1991), the Court held that a school board could be released from an injunction mandating desegregation when good faith compliance is found by the court, and vestiges of discrimination are removed as of that date. The fact that the schools had resegregated due to external factors such as residential segregation was found to be irrelevant to the Court in ending the lower court's jurisdiction over the district. This case indicates that the Court will take more of a hands-off approach toward remedying school segregation in future cases, and will be receptive to the claims of school boards that injunctive relief is no longer necessary.

iv) Restricting race-conscious efforts to combat resegregation

Declaring that "[t]he way to stop discrimination on the basis of race is to stop discriminating on the basis of race," the Supreme Court's new conservative majority sharply restricted the ability of school districts to employ race-conscious methods to block the tide of resegregation. ***Parents Involved in Community Schools v. Seattle School District No. 1***, 127 S. Ct. 2738, 2768 (2007). At issue were student assignment plans adopted by public school districts in Seattle and Louisville that relied on race to determine which schools certain children would be permitted to attend. Under these plans, Seattle classified all students as either white or nonwhite, while Louisville classified its students as either black or "other." Reaffirming its adherence to **strict scrutiny** when analyzing all race-based classifications, the Court held that the school districts bore the burden of demonstrating that their student assignment plans were **narrowly tailored to achieve a compelling government interest**. In applying that standard, the 5-vote majority held that the goal of promoting racial diversity in elementary and secondary schools is NOT a compelling government interest. 127 S. Ct. at 2753-54. In so holding, the Court rejected an effort by the school districts to invoke the affirmative-action-in-higher-education cases (discussed *infra*), where the Court has ruled that a state university DOES have a compelling government interest in achieving a diverse student body. ***Grutter v. Bollinger***, 539 U.S. 306, 325 (2003). The higher-education context is different, explained the Court, because the focus there is not solely on race; when constructing a diverse student body at the university level, race is only "part of a broader effort to achieve exposure to widely diverse people, cultures, ideas, and viewpoints." ***Parents Involved***, 127 S. Ct. at 2753. By contrast, race alone was the decisive factor in the Seattle and Louisville plans. *Id.* at 2753-54.

As beleaguered school districts try to combat resegregation, when — *if ever* — can they take race into account? On this question, the five-vote majority splintered into two irreconcilable camps: a four-vote plurality authored by Chief Justice Roberts and a solitary concurrence by Justice Kennedy. The plurality emphatically condemned "racial balancing" and any race-conscious measures by school districts. Justice Kennedy observed that the plurality opinion appeared to assert "that the Constitution requires school districts to ignore the problem of *de facto* resegregation in schooling" and "[to] accept the status quo of racial isolation in schools" — positions that he found "profoundly mistaken." 127 S. Ct. at 2791.

Justice Kennedy maintained to the contrary that, in administering public schools, "it is permissible to consider [their] racial makeup … and to adopt general policies to encourage a diverse student body, one aspect of which is its racial composition." *Id.* at 2792. If school authorities are concerned that the racial composition of a student body "interfere[s] with the objective of offering an equal educational opportunity to all of their students, they are free to devise race-conscious measures to address the problem in a general way and without treating each student in different fashion solely on the basis of a systematic, individual typing by race." *Id.* Such measures may include strategic site selection of new schools; drawing attendance zones with general recognition of neighborhood demographics; allocating resources for special programs; recruiting students and faculty in a targeted fashion; and tracking enrollments, performance, and other statistics by race. *Id.*

b) Voting

Denial of voting rights on account of race violates both the Fifteenth Amendment and the Equal Protection Clause of the Fourteenth Amendment. Since both a fundamental right and a protected class are at stake, the Court will apply the most skeptical level of review possible to governmental policies that limit the right to vote on account of race. For example, the Court struck down a Texas system of private primaries that excluded blacks from participating in the case of ***Terry v. Adams***, 345 U.S. 461 (1953), finding state action even though the primaries were nominally private. Similarly, in ***Harper v. Virginia Board of Elections,*** 383 U.S. 663 (1966), the Court struck down the use of poll taxes by the state of Virginia in part because poll taxes had historically been used to prevent African-Americans from voting in southern states.

2) Alienage — Discrimination Against Non-Citizens

Alienage classifications refer to discrimination against non-citizens. It should be noted that national origin classifications, discussed above, are different because they are based on the country where the person or his ancestors came from. Of course, the two will overlap sometimes. The general rule for alienage classifications, as for those based on national origin, is that they are subject to strict scrutiny. For example, in ***Graham v. Richardson***, 403 U.S. 365 (1971), the court applied strict scrutiny and struck down a state law denying welfare benefits to aliens because it violated equal protection. Interestingly, the Court also found the state law to be preempted by federal control over the field of immigration law.

Exceptions to Strict Scrutiny for Alienage Classifications

However, there are several exceptions where discrimination on the basis of alienage is permissible. Precisely because immigration is inherently federal and controlled by Congress, the Court will relax its standard of review when alienage classifications are created by Congress. In addition, the Court applies only rational basis review when an alienage-based classification relates to self-government and the democratic process.

Exception #1:
Deference to Federal Regulation

The Supreme Court has ruled that Congress's plenary power over immigration issues requires that the Court apply only rational basis review to federal statutes affecting aliens, even if they may be discriminatory. For example, in ***Mathews v. Diaz,*** 426 U.S. 67 (1976), the Court unanimously upheld a federal statute that denied Medicaid benefits to aliens who had lived in the country for less than five years.

Exception # 2:
Government Position Exception
The second exception to strict scrutiny for alienage classifications is that only rational basis review is required for alienage classifications relating to self-government and the democratic process. For example, in ***Foley v. Connelie***, 435 U.S. 291 (1978), the Court applied a rational basis test to uphold a state law requiring candidates for the job of police officer to be citizens. This has become known as the "government position exception," and has also been applied to uphold the exclusion of aliens from jobs as school teachers and probation officers.

3) Gender
The Court applies **intermediate** scrutiny to classifications based on **gender** and **illegitimacy**. **This level of scrutiny requires that the governmental classification be substantially related to an important governmental interest.** ***Craig v. Boren***, 429 U.S. 190 (1978). For example, in ***Craig v. Boren***, the Court struck down an Oklahoma statute prohibiting the sale of 3.2% beer to males under the age of 21 and females under the age of 18. The Court found that the government purpose, to reduce drunk driving, was important, but that the classification was not substantially related to that purpose because the statistics did not support the argument that gender could serve as a proxy for the regulation of drinking and driving.

More recently, the Court has indicated that the government must have "an exceedingly persuasive justification" for classifications based on gender. For example, in the case of ***United States v. Virginia***, 518 U.S. 515 (1996), the Court held the exclusion of women from the Virginia Military Institute to be a violation of equal protection. Virginia justified the exclusion on the basis of preserving diversity of educational opportunities for its citizens. The Court did not find the state's reason to be an exceedingly persuasive justification and ordered the state to allow women to attend VMI.

4) Non-Marital Children
The Court also applies **intermediate scrutiny** to classifications affecting **non-marital children.** For example, in ***Clark v. Jeter***, 486 U.S. 456 (1988), the Court applied intermediate scrutiny and declared unconstitutional a state law that required a non-marital child to establish paternity within six years of her birth in order later to seek support from her father. The Court stated that intermediate scrutiny is justified because children should not be penalized for matters that are beyond their control — here, whether their mother married their father.

5) Other Classifications
The Court has been asked a number of times to expand its list of suspect classifications meriting heightened scrutiny. The following is a list of classifications where the Court rejected those claims. The Court continues to apply **rational basis review** to government classifications based on the following:

a) Wealth

In ***Dandridge v. Williams***, 397 U.S. 417 (1970), the Court declined to find wealth or poverty to be a suspect classification. The Court treats government practices and policies based on wealth, or lack thereof, as economic policies, and applies rational basis review.

b) Age

Government classifications based on age merit only rational basis review. For example, in ***Massachussetts Board of Retirement v. Murgia***, 427 U.S. 307 (1976), the Court upheld a state law that required police officers to retire at age 50. The Court stated, "While the treatment of the aged in this Nation has not been wholly free of discrimination, such persons . . . have not experienced a history of unequal treatment." Moreover, the Court found that old age does not define a "discrete and insular group" meriting heightened scrutiny.

c) Mental Disability

The Court has also declared that classifications based on mental disability also merit only rational basis review. However, in the case of ***City of Cleburne v. Cleburne Living Center, Inc.***, 473 U.S. 432 (1985), the Court tacitly applied a heightened level of review to declare unconstitutional a city ordinance that required a special permit to build a group home for the mentally disabled. The Court said the policy was based on prejudice against the mentally disabled and therefore was not rational. In later cases, the Court reaffirmed that rational basis review is the appropriate standard for evaluating classifications based on mental disability.

d) Sexual Orientation

Equal protection claims by gays, lesbians, and bisexuals that challenge governmental classifications based on sexual orientation are subjected to the Court's most deferential standard: **rational basis** review. ***Romer v. Evans***, 517 U.S. 620, 631 (1996).

h. Affirmative Action or Set Asides — *Strict Scrutiny*

"Affirmative action" refers to the use of race or gender based classifications used to help, rather than discriminate against, minorities or women. The Court has upheld affirmative action on the basis of race in higher education, but has been very skeptical toward race-based preferences in every other setting. The Court has consistently held that all race-based classifications must be subjected to ***strict scrutiny*** even if their purpose is to help, rather than hinder, racial minorities.

In ***Regents of California v. Bakke***, 438 U.S. 265 (1978), the Court held that race-based classifications may be used for affirmative action in higher education, but restricted the ability of schools to use such classifications. The Court stated that race cannot be the decisive factor in admissions, but may be one of the considerations that weighs in favor of admission, as may personal talents, unique work experience, and a history of overcoming disadvantage. In a landmark decision that preserved and clarified the ***Bakke*** approach, the Supreme Court upheld a race-conscious admissions policy at the University of Michigan Law School. ***Grutter v. Bollinger***, 539 U.S. 306 (2003). In doing so, the Court confirmed (*id.* at 326) that STRICT SCRUTINY must be used in analyzing all race-based classifications — but held (*id.* at 325) that a state university's interest in achieving a diverse student body constitutes a COMPELLING STATE INTEREST for purposes of satisfying the strict scrutiny test under Equal Protection analysis.

Thus, the main issue in these higher education cases will now be whether the school's admissions policy is "narrowly tailored" to serve that compelling state interest. In ***Grutter***, the answer was ***yes***. But in its companion case, ***Gratz v. Bollinger***, 539 U.S. 244 (2003) (involving Michigan's *undergraduate* admissions policy), the answer was ***no*** — largely because the challenged policy employed a points system that awarded every minority applicant one-fifth of the total points needed for guaranteed admission merely for ***being*** a minority. This heavy-handed approach flunked the narrow tailoring requirement. By contrast, the ***Grutter*** admissions policy ***satisfied*** the narrow tailoring test because it required "a highly individualized, holistic review of each applicant's file, ... award[ing] no mechanical, predetermined diversity 'bonuses' based on race or ethnicity," 539 U.S. at 337. How do we determine whether an admissions policy is narrowly tailored? To qualify as narrowly tailored, holds ***Grutter***, a race-conscious admissions program must perform a "truly individualized" examination of every applicant, using race "in a flexible, nonmechanical way." 539 U.S. at 334. This means "that universities cannot establish quotas for members of certain racial groups or put members of those groups on separate admissions tracks. Nor can universities insulate applicants who belong to certain racial or ethnic groups from the competition for admission. Universities can, however, consider race or ethnicity more flexibly as a 'plus' factor in the context of individualized consideration of each and every applicant." 539 U.S. at 334 (citations omitted).

In another series of cases, the Court addressed the issue of whether affirmative action based on race could be used in government hiring and contracting decisions. In ***Wygant v. Jackson Board of Education***, 476 U.S. 267 (1986), the Court struck down a minority preference for teacher layoffs that had been agreed to by contract, stating that losing one's job was simply too much of a burden for the innocent white teachers to bear. In ***City of Richmond v. Croson***, 488 U.S. 469 (1989), the Court applied strict scrutiny and struck down a city of Richmond set-aside program that required city contractors to hire a certain percentage of minority subcontractors. The Court held that such practice could only be justified by a history of discrimination, which was missing in the case at hand. And most recently, in the case of ***Adarand v. Pena***, 515 U.S. 200 (1995), the Court indicated again that all race-based classifications are subject to strict scrutiny, and that affirmative action plans based on race could only be justified by remedying past discrimination.

Since strict scrutiny is almost always "fatal in fact," it is likely that courts will strike down almost all race-based affirmative action programs. In order to convince courts to uphold them, governmental agencies would have to admit to a history of past discrimination, something that they are very reluctant to do.

F. CONGRESSIONAL ENFORCEMENT OF THIRTEENTH, FOURTEENTH, AND FIFTEENTH AMENDMENTS

The Thirteenth, Fourteenth, and Fifteenth Amendments, all enacted shortly following the Civil War, contain provisions that authorize Congress to enforce them with appropriate legislation. The Court has historically read Congressional enforcement powers broadly, especially the power to enforce the Thirteenth and Fifteenth Amendments, with one significant limitation. The Court has generally held that power to enforce the Fourteenth and Fifteenth Amendments is limited to state action, although the Thirteenth Amendment does not contain such a limitation. In addition, the Court significantly restricted Congress's ability to enforce the Fourteenth Amendment in ***City of Boerne v. Flores,*** 521 U.S. 507 (1997), and in a series of cases regarding the abrogation of Eleventh Amendment immunity.

1. Thirteenth Amendment

The Thirteenth Amendment provides that "Neither slavery nor involuntary servitude, except as punishment for crime whereof the party shall have been duly convicted, shall exist within the United States, or any place subject to their jurisdiction." The Court has read Congressional power broadly, to extend not only to abolishing slavery but also the "badges and incidents" of slavery. ***Jones v. Alfred H. Mayer Co.,*** 392 U.S. 409 (1968). For example, the Court has upheld federal statutes prohibiting race discrimination in real estate transactions and contracts on the basis that such discrimination is a badge or incident of slavery.

Equally significant, the Court has interpreted the Thirteenth Amendment to authorize Congressional legislation prohibiting **private** discrimination. For example, in ***Jones***, the Court upheld the constitutionality of 42 U.S.C. §1982, which prohibits race discrimination in the sale or rental of real estate, pursuant to Congress's power to enforce the Thirteenth Amendment. The Court followed ***Jones*** in the case of ***Runyon v. McCrary,*** 427 U.S. 160 (1976), where it upheld the constitutionality of 42 U.S.C. §1981, which prohibits race discrimination in the making of contracts, and found that the statute was intended to address private discrimination. In ***Runyon***, the Court held that §1981 prohibited a private school from excluding students solely on the basis of their race.

Congress also used its Thirteenth Amendment enforcement powers to enact 42 U.S.C. §1985(3), known as the "Klu Klux Klan Act," which prohibits private conspiracies to violate civil rights. The Court upheld the constitutionality of that act, as well as its application to private activity, in ***Griffin v. Breckenridge***, 403 U.S. 88 (1971).

2. Fourteenth Amendment

Section 1 of the Fourteenth Amendment provides that "No state shall make or enforce any law which shall abridge the privileges or immunities of citizens of the United States; nor shall any State deprive any person of life, liberty, or property, without due process of law; nor deny to any person within its jurisdiction the equal protection of the laws."

Section 5 of the Fourteenth Amendment gives Congress the power to enforce these provisions and enact legislation protecting the civil rights of its citizens against interference by the states. Congress has often used this enforcement power to enact legislation protecting civil rights.

There are significant limitations on Congressional power to enforce the Fourteenth Amendment. First, it appears to be limited to state action. Second, the Court has recently indicated that it will strike down Fourteenth Amendment-based legislation if it appears that Congress, in enacting that legislation, has itself construed the Constitution in a manner at odds with Supreme Court precedent, and has thereby usurped the role of the Court as the ultimate interpreter of the Constitution.

Unlike the Thirteenth Amendment, the Court has historically held that **Congress's power to enforce the Fourteenth Amendment is limited to state action.** The Court first articulated that rule in ***The Civil Rights Cases***, 109 U.S. 3 (1883), when it held unconstitutional the Civil Rights Act of 1875, which prohibited race discrimination in private commercial activity. The Court held that the **Fourteenth Amendment cannot be used to regulate private behavior.** This ruling was upheld most recently in the case of ***United States v. Morrison***, 529 U.S. 598 (2000), in which the Court held that Congress lacked the power under the Fourteenth Amendment to enact a civil rights provision of the Violence Against Women Act, which created a cause of action for private activity.

In ***City of Boerne v. Flores***, 521 U.S. 507 (1997), the Court struck down a federal statute, the Religious Freedom Restoration Act (RFRA), as exceeding Congress's Fourteenth Amendment enforcement power. Congress relied on its Section 5 powers to enact the legislation, which purported to overturn a Supreme Court ruling on the standard to be applied to certain claims under the Free Exercise Clause. At issue was the question of whether Congress could grant new substantive rights with its Section 5 powers, or whether those powers were limited to remedying violations of the Constitution as interpreted by the Court. The ***Boerne*** Court held that RFRA went beyond Congress's enforcement powers because it was an attempt to interpret the Constitution and create new substantive rights. Stating, "Our national experience teaches that the Constitution is preserved best when each part of the government respects both the Constitution and the proper actions and determinations of the other branches," the Court struck down the Act.

3. **Fifteenth Amendment**

The Fifteenth Amendment provides, "The rights of citizens of the United States to vote shall not be denied or abridged by the United States or by any State on account of race, color, or previous condition of servitude." Congress relied on the Fifteenth Amendment to enact the Voting Rights Act of 1965, the constitutionality of which was upheld in ***South Carolina v. Katzenbach,*** 383 U.S. 301 (1965).

II. FIRST AMENDMENT FREEDOMS

The First Amendment to the United States Constitution provides:
"Congress shall make no law respecting an establishment of religion, or prohibiting the free exercise thereof; or abridging the freedom of speech, or of the press, or the right of the people peaceably to assemble, and to petition the Government for a redress of grievances."

A. FREEDOM OF SPEECH

The Text: Implications of the **Wording** of the Speech Clause

1. In sweeping fashion, the First Amendment provides that "Congress shall make no law ... abridging the freedom of speech."

2. The **wording** of this famous text raises three distinct questions about the scope of expressive freedom:

    a. Is it only the **government** — or, more narrowly, the **federal** government — that is restrained in regulating speech?

    b. Are the protections for free expression **absolute** or merely qualified?

    c. Does "freedom of speech" extend beyond the spoken or written word to embrace **nonverbal** forms of expression?

3. Is it only the **government** — or, more narrowly, the **federal** government — that is restrained in regulating speech?

    a. The First Amendment -- indeed, the whole Bill of Rights — is an express restraint on the powers of **government**.

    b. Accordingly, the First Amendment serves only to restrain **governmental** restrictions on expression.

    c. Speech regulations imposed by private actors are beyond the Amendment's reach. ***Lloyd Corp. v. Tanner***, 407 U.S. 551, 567 (1972).

    d. Private speech regulations will fall within the First Amendment's reach only if they are deemed **state action**. ***Lebron v. National Railroad Passenger Corp.,*** 513 U.S. 374, 378 (1995).

    e. Though the Amendment refers only to the **federal** government ("**Congress** shall make no law..."), it applies as well to the **states** via the 14th Amendment. ***Gitlow v. New York,*** 268 U.S. 652, 666 (1925).

4. Are the protections for free expression **absolute** or merely qualified?

   a. The Amendment's sweeping prohibition ("Congress shall make **no law**..."), suggests that it affords **absolute** protection for expressive freedom.

   b. But the Supreme Court has never embraced such a view.

   c. Even Justice Hugo Black, who declared that "no law means no law," ***New York Times Co. v. United States***, 403 U.S. 713, 717-18 (1971) (concurring opinion), retreated on many occasions from an absolutist position.

   d. First Amendment jurisprudence reflects a consistent belief that speech claims must be weighed against, and do not necessarily trump, the regulatory interests of government.

   e. Though free expression is accorded great weight in many contexts, it is never regarded as an absolute.

5. Does "freedom of speech" extend beyond the spoken or written word to embrace **nonverbal** forms of expression?

   a. By referring to "freedom of **speech**," the Amendment raises questions about the **range** of expressive activity that it protects.

   b. The Supreme Court has long employed an expansive reading of "speech," extending protection not only to oral utterances but to the written word as well — whether printed in a newspaper, held aloft on a sign, sewn onto a jacket, or transmitted through cyberspace.

   c. Protected "speech" likewise includes marching and parading, demonstrating and picketing, pamphleteering and proselytizing.

   d. It extends beyond books and newsprint to radio and television, photos and films, music and art.

   e. Even further, the freedom of "speech" extends to nonverbal **symbolic** expression, such as flag-burning and cross-burning, tree-sitting and shanty-building, armbands and sit-ins.

B. UNDERLYING THEORY: THE PHILOSOPHICAL JUSTIFICATIONS FOR PROTECTING SPEECH

1. Reasons for Protecting Speech

What are the **reasons** for protecting speech? Scholars have identified, and Supreme Court decisions fitfully reflect, **three distinct justifications**:

a. a **search-for-truth** rationale, which holds that knowledge is best obtained through the clash of rival viewpoints in an unrestricted "marketplace of ideas";

b. a **self-governance** rationale, which holds that responsive government and enlightened public policy are best achieved through unfettered political debate; and

c. a **self-fulfillment** rationale, which holds that expressive freedom is a necessary aspect of individual dignity, autonomy, and self-realization.

2. The Search-for-Truth Rationale

a. **Underlying authorities:**

1) ***Abrams v. United States***, 250 U.S. 616, 630 (1919) (Holmes, J., dissenting).

2) ***Whitney v. California***, 274 U.S. 357, 375-77 (1927) (Brandeis, J., concurring).

3) ***Terminiello v. City of Chicago***, 337 U.S. 1, 4-5 (1949) (Douglas, J., writing for the Court).

4) ***Cantwell v. Connecticut***, 310 U.S. 296, 310 (1940) (Roberts, J., writing for the Court).

b. This rationale is based upon the notion that good ideas will prevail over bad ideas when juxtaposed in the marketplace of public opinion.

c. Such a view leaves the government largely powerless to restrict access to that market; rather than acting as a content-conscious gatekeeper, the state must acquiesce in "the dissemination of noxious doctrine" [***Whitney***], even in "the expression of opinions that we loathe and believe to be fraught with death" [***Abrams***].

d. Since the clash of competing viewpoints is the path to truth [***Terminiello***], "the fitting remedy for evil counsels is good ones" [***Whitney***]. Fallacies are to be exposed through "more speech, not enforced silence" [***Whitney***].

e. This search-for-truth rationale supports a prominent feature of First Amendment jurisprudence: the Supreme Court's hostility to content-based regulation [***Cantwell***].

3. The Self-Governance Rationale

a. This rationale holds that unfettered ***political*** debate is essential to achieving responsive government and enlightened public policy.

b. Supreme Court decisions evince great respect for this rationale [e.g., ***Cohen v. California***, 403 U.S. 15, 24 (1971)], and consistently describe political speech as occupying "the core" of First Amendment protection [e.g., ***McIntyre v. Ohio Elections Commission***, 514 U.S. 334, 346 (1995)].

c. The self-governance rationale has four distinct themes:

1) Democratic self-rule entails a process of collective decision-making that requires an informed citizenry; this deliberative process functions best in an atmosphere of unfiltered debate, where the body politic is exposed to every perspective on a given issue. [Alexander Meiklejohn]

2) Unfettered discourse on public affairs prevents the entrenchment of government power and clears the path to political change. [John Hart Ely]

3) Unrestricted speech serves as a check on the abuse of power by public officials. [Vincent Blasi]

4) Fourth and finally, free speech promotes political stability by affording a safety valve for dissent. [Thomas I. Emerson]

4. The Self-Fulfillment Rationale

a. Though it supplies a strong basis for protecting speech on public affairs, the self-governance rationale offers only meager support for protecting art and literature.

b. Creative expression **is** embraced, however, by the last of the principal justifications for protecting speech: a **self-fulfillment** rationale, which holds that expressive freedom is a necessary aspect of individual dignity, autonomy, and self-realization.

c. Under this rationale, it is not just political speech but all forms of self-expression that warrant constitutional protection.

d. Broad intellectual freedom — to communicate, to inquire, to create — is a concomitant to political freedom and a precondition to realizing one's full human potential.

C. A FIVE-STEP APPROACH TO SPEECH CLAUSE ANALYSIS

1. When confronted with any issue that implicates the Speech Clause, ask the following five questions:

a. Is the regulation content-based or content-neutral?

b. If content-based, does the regulation restrict speech or compel speech?

c. If content-restrictive, is the regulation direct or indirect?

d. Does the regulation have characteristics of overbreadth, vagueness, or prior restraint?

e. Does the regulation pertain to one of the settings for which the Supreme Court has created special rules?

2. You can employ these five questions as an issue-spotting checklist whenever you are confronted with a Speech Clause problem.

3. Note that, as a prelude to engaging in this five-step inquiry, you must confirm that you are dealing with a **governmental** regulation of speech; absent **state action**, the First Amendment is not implicated. ***Lebron v. National Railroad Passenger Corp.***, 513 U.S. 374, 378 (1995).

4. The next five sections correspond, in turn, to each of the questions in this five-step inquiry. Thus, we will use the five questions as the basis for our review of Speech Clause doctrine.

D. CONTENT-BASED VERSUS CONTENT-NEUTRAL RESTRICTIONS: DIVERGING LEVELS OF JUDICIAL SCRUTINY

1. This section corresponds to Question One in our issue-spotting checklist, which inquires whether the speech regulation is content-based or content-neutral.

2. When the government regulates speech, it does so in one of two ways:
   a. restricting expressive **content**; or
   b. restricting the **time**, **place**, or **manner** of its expression.

3. Judicial hostility to the former is much greater than to the latter.

   a. "It is axiomatic," the Supreme Court has stressed, "that the government may not regulate speech based on its substantive content or the message it conveys." ***Rosenberger v. Rector & Visitors of the University of Virginia***, 515 U.S. 819, 828 (1995).

   b. In regulating speech, the government may not favor one speaker over another; discrimination against speech because of its message "is presumed to be unconstitutional." ***Rosenberger***, 515 U.S. at 828.

   c. Accordingly, the best way to begin any Speech Clause analysis is to determine whether you are looking at a content-based or a content-neutral restriction.

4. The answer to that question will dictate one of two divergent tests. In Laurence Tribe's famous formulation, they are:

   a. **"Track One" analysis** (strict scrutiny for content-based restrictions); or

   b. **"Track Two" analysis** (intermediate scrutiny for time, place, and manner restrictions).

5. **The Various Guises in Which Track One and Track Two Regulations Appear:**

   a. Impermissible content-based restrictions appear in a variety of guises; they may be grouped into five distinct categories:

      1) **First, where the government categorically suppresses or favors a particular topic or message** — as, for example, in ***Boos v. Barry***, 485 U.S. 312 (1988), where a District of Columbia statute banned the display of any sign criticizing a foreign government within 500 feet of its embassy.

      2) **Second, where the government serves as a content-conscious *gatekeeper*, selectively blocking access to a forum based on the speaker's intended *message*** — as, for example, in ***Mahoney v. Babbitt***, 105 F.3d 1452 (D.C. Cir. 1997), where the National Park Service sought to prevent anti-abortion protesters from displaying banners along the route of President Clinton's inaugural parade.

      3) **Third, where the government subjects unpopular speakers to a higher fee for using a forum** — as, for example, in ***Forsyth County v. Nationalist Movement***, 505 U.S. 123 (1992), where, under a local permit scheme, the fee for police protection could be increased if the speaker was likely to generate controversy.

      4) **Fourth, where the government withholds a service or subsidy to which the speaker would otherwise be entitled if not for his message** — as, for example, in ***Rosenberger v. Rector & Visitors of the University of Virginia***, 515 U.S. 819 (1995), where a student religious journal was denied the same subsidy for printing costs that the university furnished to all other student publications.

      5) **Fifth, where the government alters the speaker's intended message as the price for use of a forum** — as, for example, in ***Hurley v. Irish-American Gay, Lesbian & Bisexual Group of Boston***, 515 U.S. 557 (1995), where, as the price for securing their permit, the private organizers of a St. Patrick's Day parade were compelled by the government to include a contingent of gay and lesbian marchers, whose very presence would impart a message that the organizers did not wish to convey.

   b. Time, place, and manner regulations come in many forms:

      1) imposing limits on the noise level of speech;

      2) fixing caps on the number of protesters who may use a given forum;

      3) barring early-morning or late-evening demonstrations; and

      4) restricting the size or placement of signs on government property.

Note: Such regulations are frequently upheld and represent a common part of the regulatory landscape in most cities.

6. **Gauging Content Neutrality:**

a. The principal inquiry in determining content neutrality is whether the government "has adopted a regulation of speech because of disagreement with the message it conveys." ***Ward v. Rock Against Racism***, 491 U.S. 781, 791 (1989).

b. The controlling factor is the government's purpose or intent. ***Ward***, 491 U.S. at 791.

c. "A regulation that serves purposes unrelated to the content of expression is deemed neutral, even if it has an incidental effect on some speakers or messages but not others." ***Ward***, 491 U.S. at 791.

d. Government regulation of expressive activity is content-neutral so long as it is "'justified without reference to the content of the regulated speech.'" ***Ward***, 491 U.S. at 791-92 (quoting ***Clark v. Community for Creative Non-Violence***, 468 U.S. 288, 293 (1984)).

1) For an example of a speech restriction that **flunked** the content neutrality test, see ***Boos v. Barry***, 485 U.S. 312 (1988) (striking down a District of Columbia statute that criminalized the display of any sign criticizing a foreign government within 500 feet of its embassy).

e. Employing these standards, courts have held that the following speech restrictions — even though they imposed a greater hardship upon particular speakers or messages — were nonetheless content-neutral:

1) a noise regulation limiting the decibel level at Central Park concerts — even though the restriction proved especially burdensome for **rock** musicians — where the government's stated purpose was to preserve the quietude of adjacent property [***Ward v. Rock Against Racism***, 491 U.S. 781 (1989)];

2) a National Park Service ban on camping in Lafayette Park and the Mall — even though its enforcement against homeless advocates prevented them from sleeping overnight in "tent cities" near the White House — where the ban's underlying purpose was to maintain Washington's parks "in an attractive and intact condition" [***Clark v. Community for Creative Non-Violence***, 468 U.S. 288, 296 (1984)];

3) a regulation banning the overnight maintenance of any "props" on the U.S. Capitol grounds — even though it effectively thwarted a plan by homeless advocates to erect, as part of a 7-day vigil, a 500-pound clay statue of a man, woman, and child huddled over a steam grate — where the overnight ban was justified as affording the government meaningful day-to-day control over the

Capitol grounds [***Community for Creative Non-Violence v. Kerrigan***, 865 F.2d 382, 387 (D.C. Cir. 1989)]; and

4) an order banning all expressive activity within a sector of a national forest closed for logging — even though the ban's impact was entirely one-sided, since only **environmentalists** sought to protest among the trees — where the government justified its ban as protecting "health and safety and ... property" [***United States v. Fee***, 787 F. Supp. 963, 969 (D. Colo. 1992)].

f. These cases illustrate that speech restrictions will be deemed "content-neutral," even if they impinge more severely on a particular speaker or message, so long as the government can justify its regulation as serving purposes that have nothing to do with the content of speech.

g. Closely related to this theme are two strands of precedent that directly implicate the question of content neutrality:

1) the "secondary effects" doctrine; and

2) the ***O'Brien*** doctrine.

h. **The Secondary Effects Doctrine**

1) Under the secondary effects doctrine, a restriction on speech will be deemed content-neutral, even though its language is content-discriminatory, so long as the government's regulatory aim is unrelated to the speech's communicative impact. ***Young v. American Mini-Theatres, Inc.,*** 427 U.S. 50, 71 n.34 (1976).

2) The secondary effects doctrine has been successfully invoked in the regulation of adult entertainment establishments.

3) The government asserts in these cases that, even though it is singling out such establishments based on the content of the expression there, its **aim** is to address the "secondary effects" of those establishments — e.g., prostitution, declining property values, crime, and blight.

4) In ***Renton v. Playtime Theatres, Inc.,*** 475 U.S. 41, 48-49 (1986), the Court observed that such a regulatory focus "is completely consistent with our definition of 'content-neutral' speech regulations as those that are 'justified without reference to the content of the regulated speech.'"

5) The secondary effects doctrine has been largely confined to the regulation of adult entertainment; it has **not** been extended to the realm of public protest.

a) The government invoked the doctrine unsuccessfully in ***Boos v. Barry***, 485 U.S. 312 (1988), where it sought to justify a ban on the display of any sign criticizing a foreign government within 500 feet of its embassy.

b) The government argued that the ban was content-neutral because "the real concern is a secondary effect, namely, our international law obligation to shield diplomats from speech that offends their dignity." 485 U.S. at 320.

c) The Supreme Court rejected this argument and invalidated the ban under strict scrutiny, holding that "[l]isteners' reactions to speech are not the type of 'secondary effects' we referred to in ***Renton***." *Id.* at 321.

i. **The *O'Brien* Doctrine**

1) Like the secondary effects doctrine, the ***O'Brien*** doctrine erects a shield of content neutrality when the government regulates expressive activity for reasons other than its communicative impact.

2) Under ***United States v. O'Brien***, 391 U.S. 367, 377 (1968), where the government regulates **conduct** that has a communicative quality, the regulation will nevertheless survive a First Amendment challenge if the governmental **justification** for restricting the conduct is important and is unrelated to the suppression of ideas.

3) More precisely, ***O'Brien*** sets forth a **four-part test** for gauging the First Amendment validity of regulations directed at conduct comprised of both speech and non-speech elements, in cases where the government has an interest in regulating the non-speech component. Such a regulation is justified:

   a) if it is within the constitutional power of the government;

   b) if it furthers an important or substantial governmental interest;

   c) if the governmental interest is unrelated to the suppression of free expression; and

   d) if the incidental restriction on alleged First Amendment freedoms is no greater than is essential to the furtherance of that interest.

4) In ***O'Brien***, the Court upheld a federal statute criminalizing the burning of draft cards, notwithstanding a legislative history that revealed an overriding impulse to punish such conduct precisely **because** of its anti-war message, where the government justified the prohibition as furthering its administration of the Selective Service system.

j. Now that we have covered the standards for gauging content neutrality, let's turn to the differing tests that govern content-based and content-neutral regulations.

7. **"Track One" versus "Track Two" scrutiny:**

   a. The "Track One" test (for content-based restrictions on protected speech) is strict scrutiny:

      To survive judicial review, the regulation must be "necessary, and narrowly drawn, to serve a compelling state interest." ***Capitol Square Review & Advisory Board v. Pinette***, 515 U.S. 753, 761 (1995).

   b. The "Track Two" test (for time, place, and manner restrictions), definitively articulated in ***Ward v. Rock Against Racism***, 491 U.S. 781, 791 (1989), is a form of intermediate scrutiny that has three distinct prongs.

      To survive judicial scrutiny under this test, the regulation:

      1) must be content-neutral (i.e., it must be justified without reference to the content of the regulated speech);

      2) must be narrowly tailored to serve a significant governmental interest; and

      3) must leave open ample alternative channels for communicating the information.

   c. Some finer points on Track Two analysis:

      1) **The "Narrowly Tailored" Requirement in Prong #2:**

         a) ***Ward*** watered down the "narrowly tailored" requirement, stressing that time, place, and manner restrictions need not be the least restrictive or least intrusive means of achieving the government's end;

         b) Rather, the requirement of narrow tailoring is satisfied "so long as the...regulation promotes a substantial government interest that would be achieved less effectively absent the regulation." 491 U.S. at 798-99.

         c) This relaxed conception of narrow tailoring is vividly reflected in the cases.

         d) Regulations that **fail** this test invariably feature broad restraints on expressive activity — imposing, for example, sweeping prohibitions on parades, demonstrations, residential picketing, door-to-door leafleting, or public handbilling.

e) Absent this type of broad-based ban on a traditional form of expressive activity, courts routinely uphold time, place, and manner restrictions as satisfying the requirement of narrow tailoring.

2) **The "Ample Alternative Channels" Requirement in Prong #3:**

a) In real-world litigation, a speech regulation will be deemed to offend the "ample alternative channels" requirement only if it largely impairs a speaker's capacity to reach her intended audience;

b) e.g., ***Martin Luther King, Jr. Movement, Inc. v. City of Chicago,*** 419 F. Supp. 667 (N.D. Ill. 1976) (where civil rights organization sought to march through white neighborhood, its previous foray there having been curtailed when bystanders pelted the procession with rocks, bricks, and explosive devices, city officials violated the First Amendment in denying the organizers a permit for a second march through the same neighborhood, proposing instead an alternate route through an all-black neighborhood); *id.* at 673-74 (since the whole point of plaintiffs' march was to publicize and protest a pattern of violence against blacks attempting to reside in or travel through the specified neighborhood, the city's proposal for an alternate route — taking plaintiffs **away from** that neighborhood and **away from** their intended audience — was constitutionally inadequate as an alternative channel of communication).

E. RESTRICTING EXPRESSION OR COMPELLING IT: THE SPECIAL JUDICIAL HOSTILITY TO GOVERNMENT-COMPELLED SPEECH

1. This section corresponds to Question Two in our issue-spotting checklist, which inquires whether the regulation, if content-based, **restricts** speech or **compels** it.

2. If the regulation restricts rather than compels expressive content, proceed directly to Question Three, **infra**.

3. But if the regulation **compels** the utterance of, or identification with, a particular message or ideology, it will face special judicial hostility under a cluster of cases involving government-compelled speech:

   a. ***West Virginia State Board of Education v. Barnette,*** 319 U.S. 624 (1943) (striking down a mandatory flag salute and pledge of allegiance law directed at all children within the West Virginia public schools); *id.* at 642 ("[If] there is any fixed star in our constitutional constellation, it is that no official, high or petty, can prescribe what shall be orthodox in politics, nationalism, religion, or other matters of opinion or force citizens to confess by word or act their faith therein.").

b. ***Wooley v. Maynard***, 430 U.S. 705 (1977) (striking down a New Hampshire law that criminalized covering up the state motto — "Live Free or Die" — which was emblazoned on all license plates) (invoking ***Barnette***, the Court found a "freedom of mind" that protects an individual from being coerced by the state to convey an officially-mandated ideology); *id.* at 715 (the State's interest in disseminating an ideology, held the Court, "cannot outweigh an individual's First Amendment right to avoid becoming the courier for such a message").

c. ***Pacific Gas & Electric Co. v. Public Utilities Commission,*** 475 U.S. 1 (1986) (striking down a public utilities commission order that required an electric company to carry — in its own billing envelopes — messages from a consumer group with which it disagreed) (in essence, the order required the company to use its own property to disseminate a message that it opposed).

d. ***Hurley v. Irish-American Gay, Lesbian & Bisexual Group of Boston,*** 515 U.S. 557 (1995) (holding that Massachusetts could not invoke its public accommodations law to force the private organizers of a St. Patrick's Day parade to include a contingent of Irish gays and lesbians who would march under a distinct banner and convey a message that the organizers did not wish to impart; compelling the inclusion of this group effectively altered the expressive content of the organizers' parade — a type of compelled speech that violates the First Amendment).

4. Closely related to the compelled speech cases are those involving the compelled **revelation** of a speaker's identity or associational membership:

   a. ***NAACP v. Alabama***, 357 U.S. 449 (1958) (striking down enforcement of Alabama's corporate "doing-business" statute, by which the government sought to compel the disclosure of the NAACP's membership list).

   b. ***McIntyre v. Ohio Elections Commission,*** 514 U.S. 334 (1995) (striking down ban on anonymous political leafleting).

5. Not yet resolved is whether the right of anonymous expression recognized in ***McIntyre*** extends to the realm of cyberspace. **See:** ***ACLU of Georgia v. Miller,*** 977 F. Supp. 1228 (N.D. Ga. 1997) (striking down a state statute that criminalized anonymous speech on the World Wide Web).

6. Are there any situations where the Supreme Court ALLOWS the compelled revelation of speaker identity or associational membership? YES — as a permissible form of *campaign finance regulation* or as a method of policing *election referendum petitions*:

   a. *Campaign Finance Regulation:* In ***Citizens United v. Federal Election Commission***, 130 S. Ct. 876 (2010), the Court held that independent expenditures in the form of corporate political speech (e.g., a corporation pays for a TV commercial supporting a specific candidate) CAN be regulated through *disclaimer* and *disclosure* requirements that reveal the identity of the speaker. Apparently reaffirmed by ***Citizens United*** was the Court's ruling in ***Buckley v. Valeo***, 424 U.S. 1 (1976) that Congress can require the disclosure of political campaign contributions — specifically, the identity of the donor and the dollar amount conveyed.

b. *Election Referendum Petitions:* In ***Doe v. Reed***, 130 S. Ct. 2811 (2010), the Court upheld a Washington state public records statute that authorized public disclosure of the names and addresses of individuals who sign referendum petitions. The plaintiffs argued that public disclosure would chill the willingness of individuals to sign such petitions. The Court held that the state's interest in "preserving the integrity of the electoral process by combating fraud, detecting invalid signatures, and fostering government transparency and accountability," *id.* at 2819, is sufficient to justify the generally modest impact on those who sign such petitions, *id.* at 2820. But due to the procedural posture of the case, the Court's holding was limited to referendum petitions *in general* — the Court made clear that if those who sign any *particular* petition can demonstrate "a reasonable probability that the compelled disclosure [of personal information] will subject them to threats, harassment, or reprisals from either Government officials or private parties," then disclosure might well violate the First Amendment. *Id.* at 2821.

7. With the exception of the campaign finance cases (***Citizens United***, ***Buckley v. Valeo***) and the referendum petition case (***Doe v. Reed***), the Supreme Court has shown a special judicial hostility to government-compelled EXPRESSION (***Barnette***), and to government-compelled DISCLOSURE of speaker identity (***McIntyre***) or associational membership (***NAACP v. Alabama***).

8. When reviewing "[compelled] disclosure requirements in the electoral context," the Court employs a heightened standard of review that it calls "exacting scrutiny." ***Doe v. Reed***, 130 S. Ct. 2811, 2818 (2010). As enunciated by Chief Justice Roberts, "exacting" scrutiny is less demanding than strict scrutiny. "Th[e] standard," he says, "requires a substantial relation between the disclosure requirement and a sufficiently important governmental interest." ***Doe***, 130 S. Ct. at 2818 (citing ***Citizens United***, 130 S. Ct. at 914) (internal quotation marks omitted). In ***McIntyre***, Justice Stevens formulated the test quite differently, making it sound like a *souped-up* version of strict scrutiny: "[When] a law burdens core political speech, we apply '*exacting*' scrutiny, and we uphold the restriction only if it is narrowly tailored to serve an *overriding* state interest." ***McIntyre v. Ohio Elections Commission***, 514 U.S. 334, 347 (1995) (emphasis added). The current Court, at least, regards "exacting" scrutiny as falling *short* of strict scrutiny — this is apparent from Justice Thomas's dissent in ***Doe v. Reed***, where he argued that the Court *should* have applied full-blown *strict* scrutiny, not the lesser standard it employed, 130 S. Ct. at 2839 (Thomas, J., dissenting), and from the Chief Justice's majority opinion, where he acknowledged using a standard that fell short of the strict scrutiny urged by Thomas, *id.* at 2820 n.2.

F. DIRECT VERSUS INDIRECT REGULATION OF CONTENT: THE SUPREME COURT'S "CATEGORICAL" APPROACH TO DIRECT RESTRICTIONS; THE "HOSTILE AUDIENCE" SCENARIO AS AN INDIRECT RESTRICTION

1. This section corresponds to Question Three in our issue-spotting checklist, which inquires whether the regulation, if content-restrictive, is **direct** or **indirect**.

2. When the government restricts the **content** of speech, it acts in one of two ways:

    a. **directly** restricting expressive content by targeting particular topics or viewpoints; or

    b. restricting content **indirectly** by punishing a speaker for the **reaction** produced by a controversial message (the "hostile audience" cases).

3. In either context, a court will subject the restriction to heightened scrutiny. The reason for **distinguishing** between direct and indirect restrictions on speech is that each context has given birth to **distinct** lines of precedent.

4. ***Direct*** **regulation of expressive content** — examples include:

    a. statutes prohibiting the expression of certain political views (e.g., criticizing a foreign government near its embassy, soliciting votes near a polling place, expressing opposition to organized government, advocating illegal conduct to achieve political reform, calling for the government's overthrow, or urging obstruction of the war effort);

    b. statutes governing treatment of the American flag (punishing its misuse, alteration, or desecration); and

    c. statutes targeting particular types or topics of speech (e.g., fighting words, hate speech, labor speech, or threats upon the President's life).

5. ***Indirect*** **regulation of expressive content:**

    a. The **indirect** regulation of expressive content is usually accomplished by enforcing general prohibitions against undesirable **conduct** — statutes proscribing breach of the peace, disorderly conduct, disturbing a lawful meeting, or "annoying" pedestrians — as a means of punishing controversial **speech**.

    b. These are the famous "hostile audience" cases: ***Terminiello, Feiner, Cantwell, Edwards v. South Carolina, Cox v. Louisiana, Gregory v. City of Chicago.***

    c. They hold that the expression of a controversial viewpoint may not be criminalized merely because it prompts a violent reaction among onlookers enraged by the ideas expressed.

6. If you are confronted with an **indirect** restriction on expressive content (i.e., a "hostile audience" case), apply ***Terminiello*** and its progeny. [The hostile audience cases are discussed more fully in paragraph 10, below.]

7. If you are confronted with a **direct** restriction on expressive content, then consult the Supreme Court's "categorical" approach to content-based regulations. [See paragraph 8, immediately below.]

8. Direct restrictions on expressive content: categorizing speech based on its "value"

    a. When it comes to ***direct*** restrictions on expressive content, the Supreme Court has developed a "two-tiered" analytical framework, striking down such restrictions as presumptively unconstitutional unless the regulated utterance falls into one of the designated categories of "low-level" speech — categories defined in advance as being **unworthy** of full First Amendment protection.

    b. These "low-level" categories of speech are denied full First Amendment protection because, in the words of ***Chaplinsky v. New Hampshire,*** 315 U.S. 568, 571-72 (1942), they are "no essential part of any exposition of ideas," and are of only "slight social value as a step to truth."

    c. There are eight basic categories of "low-level" speech; some are utterly **unprotected** by the First Amendment, while others are **less-than-fully-protected**.

    d. The **unprotected** categories are:

        1) Advocacy of Imminent Lawless Action;

        2) Obscenity;

        3) Child Pornography;

        4) Fighting Words; and

        5) True Threats.

    e. The **less-than-fully-protected** categories are:

        1) Defamatory Statements;

        2) Commercial Speech; and

        3) the Lewd, the Profane, and the Indecent.

    f. Except for the Lewd/Profane/Indecent, each category has a recognized **test**.

g. **Advocacy of Imminent Lawless Action:**

Under ***Brandenburg v. Ohio,*** 395 U.S. 444 (1969), which jettisoned the "clear and present danger" test, such expression may be criminalized only

1) when it is **directed** to inciting or producing **imminent** lawless action,

2) and is **likely** to incite or produce such action.

h. **Obscenity:**

Under ***Miller v. California,*** 413 U.S. 15 (1973), expression will be deemed obscene, and hence utterly unprotected by the First Amendment, if it satisfies each prong in the following three-prong test:

1) Whether the average person, applying contemporary community standards, would find that the work, taken as a whole, appeals to a prurient interest in sex;

2) whether the work depicts or describes, in a patently offensive way, sexual conduct specifically defined by the applicable state law; and

3) whether the work, taken as a whole, lacks serious literary, artistic, political, and scientific value.

In a less-than-helpful elaboration of the first prong, the Supreme Court stressed that a "prurient" interest in sex is one that is "shameful or morbid" rather than "normal" and "healthy." ***Brockett v. Spokane Arcades, Inc.,*** 472 U.S. 491, 498-99 (1985).

The "patently offensive" requirement in prong two is gauged under local community standards, but the "lacks serious...value" requirement in prong three is judged under a national, objective test.

Though the private possession of obscene material is protected from prosecution, the public exhibition of such material — even in a theater open only to consenting adults — is not.

Likewise, there is no protection for importing, transporting, or distributing obscene material, even if solely for private use.

i. **Child Pornography:**

Under ***New York v. Ferber,*** 458 U.S. 747 (1982), child pornography may be criminalized under the ***Miller*** obscenity test as modified in the following ways:

1) as under ***Miller***, the prohibited conduct must be adequately defined by state statute; but, for child pornography,

2) a trier of fact need not find that the material appeals to the prurient interest of the average person;

3) it is not required that the sexual conduct portrayed be done so in a patently offensive manner; and

4) the material at issue need not be considered as a whole.

Recently, the Court confirmed that this unprotected category does not extend to "virtual" child porn; i.e., computer-generated images that were not produced by the exploitation of real children. ***Ashcroft v. Free Speech Coalition***, 535 U.S. 234 (2002). In announcing this decision, the Court reaffirmed its adherence to ***Ferber's*** definition of unprotected child porn.

If a defendant is to be criminally punished for *creating* or *possessing* child pornography, then the offending material must feature actual children and otherwise fall *within* the definition set forth in ***Ferber***. But if a defendant is to be criminally punished for *offering to sell* or *requesting to buy* child pornography, the material in question need NOT feature actual children and need NOT fall within ***Ferber's*** definition. ***United States v. Williams***, 128 S. Ct. 1830, 1842 (2008).

j. **Fighting Words:**

Under ***Chaplinsky v. New Hampshire,*** 315 U.S. 568 (1942), as limited by ***Cohen v. California,*** 403 U.S. 15 (1971), the unprotected category of "fighting words" is confined to unambiguous invitations to brawl.

k. **True Threats:**

This category of unprotected speech has received scant attention from courts and scholars. It is often overlooked. The Supreme Court has only mentioned it in a handful of cases, and has never fully developed a specific test defining its boundaries.

Nevertheless, this much is clear: "[T]hreats of violence are outside the First Amendment." ***R.A.V. v. City of St. Paul,*** 505 U.S. 377, 388 (1992).

The Court has indicated that this unprotected category should be narrowly construed. In ***Watts v. United States,*** 394 U.S. 705 (1969), the Court sided with an anti-war protester who was being prosecuted for threatening President Lyndon Baines Johnson. The defendant was arrested at an anti-war rally for telling a crowd of demonstrators: "If they ever make me carry a rifle, the first man I want to get in my sights is L.B.J." He was convicted under a federal statute that criminalizes any threat to kill or injure the President. Though the Court deemed this statute constitutional "on its face," it held that the defendant's remark was the sort of "political hyperbole" that did not constitute a "true threat." *Id.* at 708. Accordingly, it could not be deemed to fall within the statute's reach and could not be punished under the First Amendment.

Unfortunately, neither ***Watts*** nor any other Supreme Court decision has ever announced a test for "true threats." Lower courts have struggled to formulate a standard, and they have never reached agreement on a definitive test.

Nevertheless, the Second Circuit has enunciated an influential standard that has become something of a benchmark among the lower courts. In the absence of Supreme Court guidance, we may safely adopt it as our black-letter law.

A true threat, held the Second Circuit, is a threat that "on its face and in the circumstances in which it is made is so unequivocal, unconditional, immediate, and specific as to the person threatened, as to convey a gravity of purpose and imminent prospect of execution." ***United States v. Kelner,*** 534 F.2d 1020, 1027 (2d Cir. 1976), *cert. denied,* 429 U.S. 1022 (1976). A threat that falls within this definition is utterly unprotected by the First Amendment.

Some acts of cross-burning will qualify as "true threats." This is the upshot of a recent Supreme Court decision, ***Virginia v. Black***, 538 U.S. 343 (2003), ruling that Virginia's ban on cross-burning with intent to intimidate did not violate the First Amendment. The Court held that states may criminalize cross-burning so long as the state statute clearly puts the burden on prosecutors to prove that the act was intended as a threat and not as a form of symbolic expression. For doctrinal purposes, what the Court has done here is to ***include*** within the unprotected speech category of "true threats" those acts of cross-burning that are ***intended*** to intimidate a person or group of persons, placing them in fear of bodily harm or death.

l. **Defamatory Statements:**

In ***New York Times v. Sullivan,*** 376 U.S. 254 (1964), the Supreme Court took the momentous step of affording limited constitutional protection to **false** statements uttered by critics of government officials.

Recognizing "a profound national commitment to the principle that debate on public issues should be uninhibited, robust, and wide-open, and that it may well include vehement, caustic, and sometimes unpleasantly sharp attacks on government officials," *id.* at 270, the Court established qualified protection for defamatory falsehoods uttered by critics of official conduct.

The Court held that public officials are precluded from recovering damages for such statements unless they can prove that the statement was uttered "with knowledge that it was false or with reckless disregard of [its truth]." *Id.* at 279-80.

This "***Times*** malice" standard extends not only to public **officials** but to public **figures** (i.e., people who are "intimately involved in the resolution of important public questions or, by reason of their fame, shape events in areas of concern to society large").

As for libel actions by purely **private** figures, ***Times*** malice limits only the availability of **punitive** damages; compensatory damages may be awarded merely upon proof that the falsehood was published **negligently**.

The ***Times*** malice standard has been extended to other tortious statements — including false light invasions of privacy and intentional infliction of emotional distress.

m. **Commercial Speech:**

"Commercial Speech" refers to **advertising**. The prevailing test for governmental regulation of advertising is from ***Central Hudson Gas v. Public Service Commission of New York,*** 447 U.S. 557 (1980) but the Court has flatly refused, in such cases as ***Rubin v. Coors Brewing Co.,*** 514 U.S. 476 (1995) and ***44 Liquormart, Inc. v. Rhode Island***, 517 U.S. 484 (1996), to uphold "paternalistic" efforts by the government to keep consumers in the dark about the price, contents, or characteristics of a product.

The ***Central Hudson*** test has four prongs:

1) Is the advertisement protected **at all** by the First Amendment? This will depend on whether:

   a) it concerns **lawful** activity; and

   b) it is **not** misleading.

2) Next, is the asserted governmental interest "substantial"?

3) If the first two questions are answered "yes," then inquire: Did the regulation of advertising **directly advance** the asserted governmental interest?

4) If yes, then, finally, the last question is: Could the government interest be served by a more **limited** restriction on advertising? If so, the regulation is **invalid** under the First Amendment.

When applying the ***Central Hudson*** test, bear in mind the following points:

The government bears the burden of identifying a substantial interest and justifying the challenged restriction. ***Greater New Orleans Broadcasting Association, Inc. v. United States***, 527 U.S. 173, 183 (1999).

In applying the third prong ("Does the regulation ***directly advance*** the asserted governmental interest?"), remember that "[t]his burden is not satisfied by mere speculation or conjecture; rather, a governmental body seeking to sustain a restriction on commercial speech must demonstrate that the harms it recites are real and that its restriction will in fact alleviate them to a material degree." *Id.* at 188.

The Supreme Court has relaxed its enforcement of the fourth prong, no longer treating it as a "least restrictive means" test. ***Board of Trustees of SUNY v. Fox,*** 492 U.S. 469, 480 (1989) (holding that the fourth prong is satisfied where the regulation is "reasonable," with a scope "in proportion to the interest served," or where the regulation employs "a means narrowly tailored to achieve the desired objective").

n. **The Lewd/Profane/Indecent:**

1) This category does not have a specific test. Nevertheless, we **can** draw some conclusions about how such speech will be analyzed by the courts.
2) ***Cohen v. California*** tells us that the government cannot **remove** certain epithets (like "fuck") from the lexicon of public discourse.

3) ***Sable, Pacifica, Erznoznik,*** and ***Reno v. ACLU*** tell us that the Court is far more willing to uphold restrictions on lewd, profane, or indecent speech where it bombards a "captive audience."

4) ***Young, Renton, Glen Theatre,*** and ***Pap's A.M.*** indicate that when it comes to adult theaters and nude dancing, the Court will be especially deferential to governmental restrictions that are justified in terms of "secondary effects" regulation.

Watch Out!

The Court's concern about "captive audiences" being bombarded by lewd, profane, or indecent speech has prompted it to undertake a medium-by-medium examination of communications media.

It regards the broadcast medium as warranting the greatest degree of regulation because it delivers content without warning at the flick of a switch.

The Internet, on the other hand, deserves more protection from regulation because a person must take multiple steps to obtain content from it, so there is less danger of surprise exposure to unexpected content.

In its treatment of profanity and of "indecent" expression (i.e., sexually explicit speech that *falls short* of being obscene), the Supreme Court has adopted a "medium-specific" analysis, *differentiating* among the various mass communications media. ***ACLU v. Reno***, 929 F. Supp. 824, 873 (E.D. Pa. 1996) (supporting opinion of Dalzell, J.), *aff'd*, 521 U.S. 844 (1997).

The cases featuring broadcast, cable, telephone, and Internet regulation of "indecency" and profanity make clear that judicial scrutiny will *vary* depending upon the *medium* of expression.

(1) *Broadcast:* ***FCC v. Pacifica Foundation***, 438 U.S. 726, 748 (1978) (stressing the sharply diminished speech rights of broadcasters vis-à-vis their counterparts in the print media in upholding FCC's power to sanction radio station for the daytime broadcast of George Carlin's "Filthy Words" monologue).

(2) *Cable TV:* ***United States v. Playboy Entertainment Group, Inc.***, 529 U.S. 803 (2000) (using strict scrutiny to strike down a federal statute banning "signal bleed" of sexual images because such images can be fully blocked upon request by individual cable subscribers); *id.* at 804 ("There is a key difference between cable television and the broadcasting media, which is the point on which this case turns: Cable systems have the capacity to block unwanted channels on a household-by-household basis.").

(3) *Telephone:* ***Sable Communications v. FCC***, 492 U.S. 115 (1989) (striking down a federal statute that sought to eliminate the "dial-a-porn" industry); *id.* at 128 (stressing that "there is no 'captive audience' problem here; callers will generally not be unwilling listeners" because they must take affirmative steps — dialing a specific number — in order to receive the indecent communication).

(4) *Internet:* ***Reno v. ACLU***, 521 U.S. 844, 868-70 (1997) (since the factors justifying heightened regulation of the broadcast media — the history of extensive government regulation of broadcasting, the scarcity of available frequencies at its inception, and its "invasive" nature — are *not* present in cyberspace, there is no basis for qualifying the level of First Amendment scrutiny that should be applied to content-based restrictions on Internet speech; accordingly, speech in cyberspace enjoys the same enhanced protection as that reserved for books and newspapers).

The Court is *most* deferential to restrictions on *broadcasters*, and is *least* deferential to restrictions on the *print* medium and the *Internet*. ***Pacifica***; ***Reno v. ACLU***.

9. **Summing Up the Analysis of Direct, Content-Based Restrictions on Speech**

a. Bear in mind that if you are confronted with a direct, content-based restriction on speech, you would normally analyze it under the "Track One" strict scrutiny test: To survive judicial review, the regulation must be "necessary, and narrowly drawn, to serve a compelling state interest." ***Capitol Square Review & Advisory Board v. Pinette,*** 515 U.S. 753, 761 (1995).

b. But before applying strict scrutiny, you should always check to see if the regulated speech falls into one of the foregoing "low-level" categories of expression:

1) Advocacy of Imminent Lawless Action
2) Obscenity
3) Child Pornography
4) Fighting Words
5) True Threats
6) Defamatory Statements
7) Commercial Speech
8) The Lewd/Profane/Indecent

c. If the regulated speech DOES fall into one of those unprotected or less-than-fully-protected categories, then DO NOT apply strict scrutiny. Instead, apply the specific test that prevails in the applicable category.

d. Bear in mind, finally, that if the regulation you are analyzing is NOT content-based, you should drop down from "Track One" analysis to "Track Two" analysis, employing the prevailing test for time, place, and manner restrictions set forth in ***Ward v. Rock Against Racism,*** 491 U.S. 781, 791 (1989), a form of intermediate scrutiny that has three distinct prongs. To survive judicial scrutiny under this test, the regulation:

1) must be content-neutral (i.e., it must be justified without reference to the content of the regulated speech);

2) must be narrowly tailored to serve a significant governmental interest; and

3) must leave open ample alternative channels for communicating the information.

10. **Indirect** Regulation of Content: **The "Hostile Audience" Cases**

a. In contrast to **direct** regulation of expressive content, which is usually accomplished by provisions affirmatively suppressing a particular message, content is regulated **indirectly** by punishing a speaker for the **reaction** to her controversial speech.

b. These are the so-called "hostile audience" cases, which hold that the expression of a controversial viewpoint may not be criminalized merely because it prompts a violent response amongst onlookers enraged by the ideas expressed:

1) ***Terminiello v. City of Chicago,*** 337 U.S. 1 (1949).

a) The Supreme Court here reversed a breach-of-the-peace conviction of a widely vilified speaker whose anti-Semitic and racially inflammatory speech produced a near riot.

b) Calling his antagonists "'slimy scum,' 'snakes,' [and] 'bedbugs,'" *id.* at 26, the defendant delivered a venomous speech to an auditorium packed with 800 supporters, *id.* at 3, while outside, straining against a cordon of police, "'a surging, howling mob'" of 1000 people "'hurl[ed] epithets at those who would enter and tried to tear their clothes off,'" *id.* at 16.

c) At trial, the defendant's conviction followed a jury instruction that authorized punishment for speech that "'stirs the public to anger, invites dispute, brings about a condition of unrest, or creates a disturbance.'" *Id.* at 3.

d) In one of the most famous passages in all of First Amendment law, Justice Douglas, writing for the Court, held that this jury instruction offended the Constitution — because "a **function** of free speech under our system of government is to invite dispute." *Id.* at 4 (emphasis added).

2) ***Cantwell v. Connecticut,*** 310 U.S. 296 (1940).

a) Setting aside breach-of-the-peace conviction of defendant, a Jehovah's Witness, who, in the course of his sidewalk proselytizing, incensed passers-by in playing a phonograph record that expressed virulently anti-Catholic sentiments.

b) Holding that defendant, whose conduct was neither truculent nor abusive, could not be convicted for breaching the peace based on the hostile reaction of his audience to the sentiments he was disseminating.

c) Observing that sharp differences arise in religion and politics — and that, in an effort to persuade, speakers sometimes resort to **exaggeration** and **vilification**. But these excesses must be tolerated to vouchsafe our liberty of expression.

c. The Supreme Court reached a contrary result in ***Feiner v. New York,*** 340 U.S. 315 (1951) (**upholding** the disorderly conduct conviction of a college student who, standing atop a soapbox and using a loudspeaker, delivered a street corner harangue to a crowd of 80 people in which his derogatory remarks about President Truman, the American Legion, the Mayor of Syracuse, and other local officials inspired a hostile audience reaction).

1) In dissent, Justice Black observed: "It is neither unusual nor unexpected that some people at public street meetings mutter, mill about, push, shove, or disagree, even violently, with the speaker. Indeed, it is rare where controversial topics are discussed that an outdoor crowd does not do some or all of these things." *Id.* at 325-26.

2) Justice Black went on to assert that police have a **duty to protect** the unpopular speaker.

3) Such a duty — though never expressly adopted or rejected by a Supreme Court majority — HAS been consistently recognized by the lower federal courts:

a) ***Sabel v. Stynchcombe,*** 746 F.2d 728 (11th Cir. 1984) (overturning refusal-to-disperse convictions of Revolutionary Communist Party demonstrators who, in the course of a May Day Rally, inspired a hostile reaction by 200 onlookers); *id.* at 731 & n.7 (recognizing that police have a duty to protect unpopular speakers confronted by a hostile crowd); *id.* at 730-31 (concluding that "the 'shouting,' 'shoving,' and 'cursing'" that witnesses observed among the 200 onlookers "provided an insufficient basis for governmental restriction of protected speech").

b) ***Glasson v. City of Louisville,*** 518 F.2d 899 (6th Cir. 1975) (sustaining § 1983 action by solitary anti-Nixon protester whose sign was destroyed by police at the behest of hostile onlookers); *id.* at 905-06 (holding that police not only violated the First Amendment by destroying Plaintiff's sign but had an affirmative duty to protect her from the hostile crowd).

d. ***Feiner's*** continued vitality remains in some doubt, given the Civil Rights Trilogy of the 1960s: ***Edwards v. South Carolina,*** 372 U.S. 229 (1963); ***Cox v. Louisiana,*** 379 U.S. 536 (1965); and ***Gregory v. Chicago,*** 394 U.S. 111 (1969):

1) ***Edwards*** set aside breach-of-the peace convictions of 187 civil rights protesters who, after marching peacefully on a sidewalk around the South Carolina State House grounds, refused a police order to disperse and, after 15 minutes of singing and speechmaking, were arrested. This demonstration — in which marchers carried placards reading "Down with Segregation," "I Am Proud to be a Negro," and similar messages — produced a tense crowd of 200 to 300 onlookers. The Court held that the state cannot criminalize "the peaceful expression of unpopular views." 379 U.S. at 237.

2) ***Cox*** set aside the breach-of-the-peace conviction of a civil rights activist who led a peaceful march by 2000 students to a courthouse where, with songs, prayers, and speeches, they protested the arrest and incarceration of fellow activists, who were being held in the adjacent jail. Urging his charges to dine at nearby segregated lunch counters, the defendant prompted some "muttering" and "grumbling" among the 100 to 300 white onlookers positioned across the street. The demonstration ended in chaos when police fired tear gas at the students after defendant refused a dispersal order. The Court struck down — on overbreadth grounds — Louisiana's breach-of-the-peace statute, which "would allow persons to be punished merely for peacefully expressing unpopular views." 379 U.S. at 551.

3) ***Gregory*** overturned the disorderly conduct convictions of 85 civil rights protesters whose march to and picketing before the mayor's residence produced a hostile reaction by 1000 onlookers. The Court held that the First Amendment barred the protesters' convictions where, pelted by rocks and eggs, they remained peaceful throughout their demonstration and were arrested only after refusing a police dispersal demand prompted solely by the onlookers' unruliness.

e. **The Heckler's Veto Doctrine**

1) The underlying rationale of the hostile audience cases is to prevent a "**heckler's veto**" of minority opinions.

2) The idea here is to give minority viewpoints a chance to enter the marketplace of ideas and gain adherents.

f. **How Do We Analyze a Hostile Audience Case?**

1) When confronted with a hostile audience scenario, remember that: (a) a speaker cannot be punished because of an angry reaction to her ideas; (b) police have a duty to protect the unpopular speaker; and (c) if police are faced with an ongoing and uncontrollable crowd reaction, they will take the unpopular speaker into temporary protective custody, but they may not jail or prosecute her.

2) Remember these points:

a) It is presumptively unconstitutional for the State to silence or punish someone simply because the content of their expression is offensive or provocative. ***Texas v. Johnson,*** 491 U.S. 397 (1989).

b) Though ***Feiner*** has never been overruled, its continued vitality is questionable in light of the Court's subsequent decisions in ***Edwards, Cox,*** and ***Gregory*** (the "Civil Rights Trilogy").

G. OTHER REGULATORY FLAWS: PRIOR RESTRAINT, OVERBREADTH, AND VAGUENESS

This section corresponds to Question Four in our issue-spotting checklist, which inquires whether the regulation has characteristics of overbreadth, vagueness, or prior restraint.

1. The doctrines of overbreadth, vagueness, and prior restraint are united by one common characteristic: each is concerned with an impermissible METHOD of regulating speech.

2. These doctrines focus not on the ***content*** of speech but on the regulatory MEANS employed by the government in restricting it.

3. The **overbreadth** doctrine may be invoked to strike down restrictions on speech that are worded in such a way that even protected expression is left vulnerable to punishment.

4. The **vagueness** doctrine may be invoked to strike down restrictions on speech that are worded in such a way that citizens cannot reasonably discern what is prohibited.

5. In reaction to the now-vilified press licensing systems of the 16th and 17th centuries, the doctrine of **prior restraint** imposes severe limits on the power of government to regulate speech BEFORE it is uttered or published.

6. **The Overbreadth Doctrine:**

   a. This doctrine is designed to invalidate speech restrictions that are so sweeping in scope that even **protected** expression is rendered vulnerable to punishment.

   b. Examples of speech restrictions held to be unconstitutionally overbroad:

      1) ***Board of Airport Commissioners of Los Angeles v. Jews for Jesus, Inc.,*** 482 U.S. 569 (1987) (striking down, on overbreadth grounds, a regulation prohibiting any person "to engage in First Amendment activities within the Central Terminal Area at Los Angeles International Airport"); *id.* at 575 (striking down the regulation because "it prohibits even talking and reading, or the wearing of campaign buttons or symbolic clothing").

      2) ***City of Houston v. Hill,*** 482 U.S. 451 (1987) (striking down — as facially overbroad — an ordinance prohibiting speech that "in any manner" interrupts a police officer in performing his duties; the ordinance was so broadly worded that it was violated every day and effectively gave police unfettered discretion to arrest individuals for words or conduct that merely annoyed or offended them).

      3) ***Reno v. ACLU,*** 521 U.S. 844 (1997) (striking down -- as facially overbroad — provisions of the Communications Decency Act, a federal statute that criminalized the Internet transmission of "indecent" materials to persons under the age of 18); *id.* at 874 ("In order to deny minors access to potentially harmful speech, the [Act] effectively suppresses a large amount of speech that adults have a constitutional right to receive and to address to one another.").

   c. What are the **justifications** for the overbreadth doctrine?

      1) concerns about the **chilling** effect of overbroad prohibitions on speech; and

      2) a recognition that the broader the statute, the broader will be the **discretion** enjoyed by government officials to engage in **selective** enforcement.

   d. Important **procedural** aspects of the overbreadth doctrine:

      1) permits **facial** rather than as-applied challenges;

      2) **relaxes** the normal **standing** rules governing who may bring a constitutional challenge;

3) is limited by the power of a court to save an overbroad statute through a "**narrowing construction**"; and

4) is limited by the requirement of "**substantial**" overbreadth.

e. **Facial** challenges:

1) The doctrine authorizes a **facial** challenge to an overbroad speech restriction that, if successful, results in the statute's TOTAL invalidation.

2) This is very different, and far more devastating, than the result of an **as-applied** challenge.

3) A successful facial challenge effectively wipes the offending statute right out of the codebooks. But an as-applied challenge, even if successful, leaves the statute in effect, and bars its enforcement only in a certain manner or under certain circumstances.

4) Thus, when a speech restriction is declared facially overbroad, its enforcement by the government in **any** context is impermissible.

5) A footnote: Under the First Amendment, overbreadth is not the only sort of claim that may be asserted as a facial challenge. "There are two quite different ways in which a statute or ordinance may be considered invalid 'on its face' — either because it is unconstitutional in every conceivable application [e.g., content-based restrictions on protected speech], or because it seeks to prohibit such a broad range of protected [expression] that it is unconstitutionally 'overbroad.'" ***Members of the City Council of Los Angeles v. Taxpayers for Vincent,*** 466 U.S. 789, 796 (1984).

f. **Relaxation** of the normal **standing** rules:

1) The overbreadth doctrine authorizes a **relaxation** of the normal **standing** rules governing who may bring a constitutional challenge.

2) The Supreme Court "has altered its traditional rules of standing to permit -- in the First Amendment area — 'attacks on overly broad statutes with no requirement that the person making the attack demonstrate that his own [speech] could not be [punished if the] statute [were] drawn with the requisite narrow specificity.' Litigants, therefore, are permitted to challenge a statute not because their own rights of free expression are violated, but because of a judicial prediction or assumption that the statute's very existence may cause others not before the court to refrain from constitutionally protected speech or expression." ***Broadrick v. Oklahoma,*** 413 U.S. 601, 612 (1973) (quoting ***Dombrowski v. Pfister,*** 380 U.S. 479, 486 (1965)).

3) ***Gooding v. Wilson,*** 405 U.S. 518 (1972) is a vivid example of the extent to which the normal rules of standing are relaxed in overbreadth challenges. It shows why the Supreme Court considers the overbreadth doctrine to be "strong medicine." ***Osborne v. Ohio,*** 495 U.S. 103, 122 (1990); ***Broadrick,*** 413 U.S. at 613.

4) In ***Gooding***, the Supreme Court sustained an overbreadth challenge to a Georgia statute that criminalized a spectrum of statements far broader than fighting words ("opprobrious words or abusive language tending to cause a breach of the peace," *id.* at 519) — but it did so in a case where the person challenging the statute likely HAD uttered fighting words.

5) ***Gooding*** stemmed from a clash between police and anti-war demonstrators at an army induction center. When police attempted to move the defendant away from the facility's entrance, a scuffle ensued in which he said to the officers: "You son of a bitch, I'll choke you to death!" and "White son of a bitch, I'll kill you!" and "You son of a bitch, if you ever put your hands on me again, I'll cut you all to pieces!" 405 U.S. at 520 n.1.

6) Since these words likely fall within the definition of fighting words, it would have been constitutionally permissible to punish this defendant under an appropriately narrow statute.

7) But the Georgia statute was not narrow — and because it swept so far beyond the scope of "fighting words," it was vulnerable to an overbreadth challenge. What ***Gooding*** shows is that STANDING to assert such a challenge is available even to someone who did ***not*** engage in constitutionally protected speech and who would **not** have escaped conviction under an appropriately narrow statute.

8) And what is the **reason** for these relaxed standing rules? "[They are] deemed necessary," observed Justice Brennan, "because persons whose expression *is* constitutionally protected may well refrain from exercising their rights for fear of criminal sanctions [under] a statute susceptible of application to protected expression." ***Gooding,*** 405 U.S. at 521 (emphasis added).

g. "**Narrowing**" constructions:

1) The overbreadth doctrine is limited by the power of courts to save an overbroad statute through the issuance of a "**narrowing construction**."

2) Such a construction effectively **rewrites** the statute, declaring its scope to be more limited than what its sweeping language would suggest, and identifying the constricted range of circumstances to which it may henceforth be applied.

3) The Supreme Court has cautioned against the wholesale use of this approach, observing that a narrowing construction should be imposed on a statute "only if it is 'readily susceptible' to such a construction." ***Reno v. ACLU***, 521 U.S. 844,

884 (1997) (quoting ***Virginia v. American Booksellers Association, Inc.,*** 484 U.S. 383, 397 (1988)).

4) The appropriate source of a narrowing construction depends on the statute's origin: federal courts are free to narrow **federal** statutes, ***Reno v. ACLU***, 521 U.S. 844, 884 (1997), but **state** legislation should be narrowed by the courts of that state, ***Gooding v. Wilson,*** 405 U.S. 518, 520 (1972); ***Erznoznik v. City of Jacksonville,*** 422 U.S. 205, 216 (1975).

5) When, in ***Gooding v. Wilson,*** 405 U.S. 518 (1972), the Supreme Court invoked the overbreadth doctrine to strike down Georgia's "abusive language" statute, it observed that the Georgia courts **had not** issued the sort of narrowing construction that might have saved the statute. *Id.* at 524.

h. "**Substantial**" overbreadth:

1) The Supreme Court cut back on the doctrine's availability by imposing the requirement of "**substantial**" overbreadth. ***Broadrick v. Oklahoma,*** 413 U.S. 601, 615-16 (1973).

2) What is meant by "substantial" overbreadth is less than clear. Straining to elaborate, the Court has observed: "The concept of 'substantial overbreadth' is not readily reduced to an exact definition. It is clear, however, that the mere fact that one can conceive of some impermissible applications of a statute is not sufficient to render it susceptible to an overbreadth challenge. On the contrary....there must be a realistic danger that the statute itself will significantly compromise recognized First Amendment protections of parties not before the Court for it to be facially challenged on overbreadth grounds." ***Members of the City Council of Los Angeles v. Taxpayers for Vincent,*** 466 U.S. 789, 800-01 (1984).

3) An example of how the Court applies the requirement of "substantial" overbreadth is ***New York v. Ferber,*** 458 U.S. 747 (1982), where it rejected an overbreadth challenge to a statute that prohibited persons from knowingly promoting a sexual performance by a child under the age of 16.

4) While recognizing that this statute might reach some protected expression (like medical textbooks or pictorials in National Geographic), the Court observed: "[W]e seriously doubt...that these arguably impermissible applications...amount to more than a tiny fraction of the materials within the statute's reach." 458 U.S. at 773.

5) Thus, a statute will be deemed unconstitutionally overbroad only when, within the range of its potential applications, a substantial number entail protected expression. **See:** ***Ferber***, 458 U.S. at 771; ***Regan v. Time, Inc.,*** 468 U.S. 641, 650-51 (1984).

7. **The Vagueness Doctrine:**

   a. The vagueness doctrine may be invoked to strike down restrictions on speech that are worded in such a way that citizens cannot reasonably discern what is prohibited.

   b. A speech restriction is void for vagueness unless it gives a "person of ordinary intelligence a reasonable opportunity to know what is prohibited, so that he may act accordingly." ***Grayned v. City of Rockford,*** 408 U.S. 104, 108 (1972). *Accord:* ***Holder v. Humanitarian Law Project***, 130 S. Ct. 2705, 2718-19 (2010) (rejecting vagueness challenge to federal statute that imposes a criminal ban on providing material support, in the form of "personnel" or "training," to any organization that is designated by the Secretary of State as a foreign terrorist organization). In ***Holder***, the Court phrased the vagueness test as follows: "'A conviction fails to comport with due process [due to vagueness] if the statute under which it is obtained fails to provide a person of ordinary intelligence fair notice of what is prohibited, or is so standardless that it authorizes or encourages seriously discriminatory enforcement.'" 130 S. Ct. at 2718-19 (quoting ***United States v. Williams***, 553 U.S. 285, 304 (2008)).

   c. In ***Grayned***, 408 U.S. at 108-09, the Supreme Court identified three distinct policy grounds for striking down vague laws:

      1) Vague laws may trap the innocent by not providing fair warning of what is proscribed.

      2) Vague laws effectively delegate enforcement discretion to policemen, judges, and juries, freeing them to act on an ad hoc and subjective basis, with the attendant dangers of arbitrary and discriminatory application.

      3) When directed at expressive activity, vague laws can inhibit the exercise of First Amendment freedoms. Indeed, vagueness can have the same **effect** as overbreadth, prompting citizens to steer a wide path around the perceived prohibition.

   d. In ***Smith v. Goguen,*** 415 U.S. 566 (1974), the Court sustained a vagueness challenge to a Massachusetts statute that criminalized publicly treating the American flag "contemptuously."

   e. The Court observed that any "unceremonial" use of the flag might be regarded by some as "contemptuous," but that casual treatment of the flag (as "an object of youth fashion and high camp") had become commonplace. 415 U.S. at 573-74.

   f. Given the prevalence of these widely divergent views, a statute criminalizing the "contemptuous" use of the flag was so vague that police, courts, and juries were free to enforce it under their **own** preferences for how the flag should be treated. *Id.* at 574-75. Accordingly, the Court ruled the statute void for vagueness.

g. In contrast to an overbreadth challenge, where the statute must be shown to reach a **substantial** number of impermissible applications, ***Ferber***, 458 U.S. at 771, a vagueness challenge will fail unless the statute is shown to be "impermissibly vague in **all** of its applications." ***Village of Hoffman Estates v. Flipside, Hoffman Estates, Inc.,*** 455 U.S. 489, 497 (1982).

h. Also in contrast to the overbreadth doctrine, vagueness challenges do **not** enjoy the same relaxed rules on standing. ***Holder v. Humanitarian Law Project,*** 130 S. Ct. 2705, 2719 (2010).

8. **The Doctrine of Prior Restraint:**

a. In reaction to the now-vilified press licensing systems of the 16th and 17th centuries, the doctrine of prior restraint imposes severe limits on the power of government to regulate speech BEFORE it is uttered or published.

b. Prior restraints come in two forms:

1) speech-restrictive **injunctions**; and

2) **licensing** systems that require a permit or fee as a prerequisite to engaging in expressive activity.

c. Speech-restrictive **injunctions**:

1) There are four basic points to bear in mind with regard to speech-restrictive injunctions:

a) A **flat, pre-publication gag order** is presumptively unconstitutional.

b) **Injunctions** that impose time, place, or manner restrictions are subject to a heightened form of intermediate scrutiny.

c) **Speech-restrictive injunctions** must not be granted **ex parte**, and their restraints must be limited to the narrowest possible scope.

d) Under the **"collateral bar" rule,** speech-restrictive injunctions **must** be obeyed even if they are unconstitutional.

Let's take a closer look at each of these four points:

2) **A flat, pre-publication gag order is presumptively unconstitutional:**

a) ***Nebraska Press Association v. Stuart,*** 427 U.S. 539 (1976) (striking down a gag order on press coverage of a murder trial; the injunction, issued by the trial judge, barred newspapers and broadcasters from reporting any confession by, or inculpatory information about, the accused); *id.* at 558 ("Any prior restraint on expression comes to this Court with a 'heavy presumption' against its constitutional validity."); *id.* at 562 (the test: "[whether] the gravity of the 'evil' [posed by publication], discounted by its improbability, justifies such invasion of free speech as is necessary to avoid the danger").

b) ***New York Times v. United States,*** 403 U.S. 713 (1971) (striking down injunctions that barred the New York Times and Washington Post from publishing excerpts from the "Pentagon Papers," a top secret Defense Department study of the Vietnam War).

c) ***Near v. Minnesota,*** 283 U.S. 697 (1931) (striking down an injunction that perpetually enjoined the Saturday Press from publishing any "malicious, scandalous, or defamatory" material; the paper had been sharply critical of the Minneapolis police chief, accusing him of corruption).

d) **But see *United States v. The Progressive, Inc.,*** 467 F. Supp. 990 (W.D. Wis. 1979) (**granting** preliminary injunction against magazine that sought to discredit the government's system of classification and secrecy by publishing an article revealing that much of the information necessary for constructing an H-Bomb was already contained in publicly available literature).

3) Injunctions that impose time, place, or manner restrictions are subject to a heightened form of intermediate scrutiny — under a test that is slightly more stringent than that for legislation:

a) Observing that "[i]njunctions ... carry greater risks of censorship and discriminatory application than do general ordinances," the Supreme Court held in 1994 that speech-restrictive injunctions should be subjected by appellate courts to more "stringent" First Amendment scrutiny than comparable legislation — that, "when evaluating a content-neutral **injunction**, we think that our standard time, place, and manner analysis is not sufficiently rigorous." ***Madsen v. Women's Health Center, Inc.,*** 512 U.S. 753, 764-65 (1994) (emphasis added).

b) Announcing a new standard of review for content-neutral **injunctions**, the Court held that, rather than inquiring whether the order is narrowly tailored to serve a significant governmental interest, "[w]e must ask instead whether the challenged provisions of the injunction **burden no more speech than necessary** to serve a significant government interest." *Id.* at 765.

4) Speech-restrictive injunctions must not be issued **ex parte**, and their restraints must be limited to the narrowest possible scope:

a) These twin teachings were emphatically delivered in ***Carroll v. President & Commissioners of Princess Anne***, 393 U.S. 175 (1968), where the Supreme

Court struck down a 10-day injunction, issued **ex parte**, that banned further demonstrations by a white supremacist group.

b) The Court suggested that **ex parte** speech restrictions are presumptively unconstitutional; this is because, by definition, their issuance takes place without the crucial benefit of evidentiary input from both sides of the dispute, *id.* at 183, and the procedural safeguards necessary for sustaining a prior restraint are thus entirely lacking, *id.* at 180-82.

c) The injunction was offensive to the First Amendment not only for its **ex parte** issuance but also for its broad scope (it enjoined the group from holding meetings or rallies anywhere in the county "'which will tend to disturb and endanger'" the local citizenry, *id.* at 177).

d) On this point, the Court stressed that speech-restrictive injunctions "must be couched in the narrowest terms that will accomplish the pinpointed objective permitted by constitutional mandate and the essential needs of public order." *Id.* at 184.

5) Under the "collateral bar" rule, speech-restrictive injunctions **must** be obeyed even if they are unconstitutional:

a) The collateral bar rule requires obedience to injunctive orders. ***GTE Slyvania v. Consumers Union,*** 445 U.S. 375, 386 (1980).

b) By engaging in expressive activity in defiance of such an injunction, a speaker places herself in contempt of court — and, under the collateral bar rule, the injunction's unconstitutionality is **no defense** to the contempt citation. Randy Barnett, ***The Puzzle of Prior Restraint,*** 29 Stan. L. Rev. 539, 553 (1977).

c) An example of this is ***Walker v. City of Birmingham,*** 388 U.S. 307 (1967), where the Supreme Court upheld the criminal contempt convictions of eight black ministers who defied a temporary restraining order requiring them to secure a permit before conducting a civil rights march.

d) Though the ***Walker*** Court suggested that the injunction might well have been constitutionally suspect, *id.* at 318-19, it refused to reach that issue, holding that the ministers, while free to challenge the injunction in court, were **not** free to defy it, *id.* at 319-21.

e) One unfortunate effect of the collateral bar rule is that prospective speakers, confronted by an unconstitutional injunction, can be silenced for months on end while they pursue the path of judicial review.

d. **Licensing** systems that require a permit or fee as a prerequisite to engaging in expressive activity.

1) Of the two basic forms of prior restraint, speech-restrictive **injunctions** are one type, while speech-restrictive **licensing** schemes are the other.

2) Such licensing schemes will run afoul of the First Amendment if they fail to limit:

   a) the licensor's **discretion** in issuing a permit or fee; or

   b) the **time frame** for issuing a license.

3) In ***FW/PBS, Inc. v. City of Dallas,*** 493 U.S. 215 (1990), the Supreme Court identified "two evils" in speech licensing schemes "that will not be tolerated" — vesting "unbridled discretion" in the licensing authority, and "fail[ing] to place limits on the time within which the decision maker must issue the license." *Id.* at 225-26.

4) Let's examine these "two evils" in turn.

5) **Vesting "unbridled discretion" in the licensing authority**

   a) Courts have consistently invalidated permit schemes vesting government officials with unfettered discretion to forbid or allow certain speech activities:

      i) ***City of Lakewood v. Plain Dealer Publishing Co.,*** 486 U.S. 750 (1988) (permit to place news racks on public property).

      ii) ***Southeastern Promotions, Ltd. v. Conrad,*** 420 U.S. 546 (1975) (permit to use city auditorium).

      iii) ***Shuttlesworth v. City of Birmingham,*** 394 U.S. 147 (1969) (parade permit).

      iv) ***Hague v. CIO,*** 307 U.S. 496 (1939) (permit for public meetings and demonstrations).

      v) ***Kunz v. New York,*** 340 U.S. 290 (1951) (permit for sidewalk preaching).

      vi) ***Schneider v. New Jersey,*** 308 U.S. 147 (1939) (leafleting permit).

   b) Any scheme that vests arbitrary discretion in the licensing official "has the potential for becoming a means of suppressing a particular point of view." ***Heffron v. International Society for Krishna Consciousness, Inc.,*** 452 U.S. 640, 649 (1981).

   c) Accordingly, a permit scheme will survive constitutional scrutiny only if it employs content-neutral criteria, and only if it contains "narrowly drawn, reasonable, and definite standards for the officials to follow." ***Niemotko v. Maryland,*** 340 U.S. 268, 271 (1951).

d) Without such standards, "post hoc rationalizations by the licensing official and the use of shifting or illegitimate criteria are far too easy, making it difficult for courts to determine in any particular case whether the licensor is permitting favorable, and suppressing unfavorable, expression." ***City of Lakewood v. Plain Dealer Publishing Co.,*** 486 U.S. 750, 758 (1989).

e) Closely akin to these "unfettered discretion" cases are those in which the permit scheme allows licensing officials to consider either the controversial nature of a speaker's message or its potential for inspiring a hostile response.

f) These schemes are struck down just as readily — and for the same reason — as the schemes affording unbridled discretion. In both contexts, the First Amendment flaw is the same: the right to speak is left to hinge on the ***popularity*** of one's message.

g) The permit schemes in this line of precedent are of two (equally fatal) types:

   i) those allowing the licensor to forbid or restrict speech activities based on concerns that the speaker's message will inspire a hostile response (e.g., ***Williams v. Wallace,*** 240 F. Supp. 100 (M.D. Ala. 1965) (ordering Alabama to permit Martin Luther King Jr.'s march from Selma to Montgomery); ***Village of Skokie v. National Socialist Party of America,*** 366 N.E.2d 347 (Ill. App. 1977) (declining to enjoin Nazi march through Illinois suburb populated by Holocaust survivors)); and

   ii) those allowing the licensor to charge a higher police-protection fee based on the anticipated level of hostility among onlookers (e.g., ***Forsyth County v. Nationalist Movement,*** 505 U.S. 123, 134-35 (1992) (since "[t]hose wishing to express views unpopular with bottle-throwers…may have to pay more for their permit," the Court struck the scheme down, asserting: "Speech cannot be financially burdened, any more than it can be punished or banned, simply because it might offend a hostile mob.")).

6) **Failing to place limits on the time frame for issuing a license**

a) Courts will treat as "a species of unbridled discretion" any failure by a licensing scheme to place limits on the **time frame** for issuing a permit. ***FW/PBS,*** 493 U.S. at 223-24.

b) A licensing scheme may run afoul of this requirement in one of two ways:

i) by failing to afford prompt processing of permit applications or prompt judicial review of permit denials (e.g., ***Freedman v. Maryland,*** 380 U.S. 51, 58-60 (1965)); and

ii) by imposing advance registration requirements that build into the application process a lengthy delay before the licensee may speak (e.g., ***NAACP v. City of Richmond,*** 743 F.2d 1346 (9th Cir. 1984) (black man's death in police custody prompted immediate plans for a protest march, but city officials thwarted the march by invoking a 20-day advance registration requirement in their parade permit ordinance — struck down as effectively "outlaw[ing] spontaneous expression").

7) **Permit schemes governing public parks**
The Supreme Court has held that the "extraordinary procedural safeguards" required by ***Freedman v. Maryland***, 380 U.S. 51 (1965), which were designed for motion picture censorship schemes, do **not** apply to municipal permit schemes governing expressive access to public parks. ***Thomas v. Chicago Park District***, 534 U.S. 316 (2002).

a) Specifically, this means that park use permit schemes do **not** run afoul of the prior restraint doctrine if they fail to afford prompt judicial review of permit denials.

b) But ***Thomas*** makes clear that municipal permit schemes governing expressive access to public parks **remain** vulnerable to constitutional challenge if they vest the licensing official with **unfettered discretion** to grant or deny the application.

8) **Permit schemes governing door-to-door advocacy**
The Supreme Court struck down — as applied to religious proselytizing, anonymous political speech, and the distribution of handbills — an ordinance that made it a misdemeanor to engage in door-to-door advocacy without first registering with the mayor and obtaining a permit. ***Watchtower Bible & Tract Society v. Stratton***, 536 U.S. 150 (2002).

H. SPECIAL RULES FOR SPECIAL SETTINGS

This section corresponds to Question Five in our issue-spotting checklist, which inquires whether the speech regulation pertains to one of the settings for which the Supreme Court has created special rules.

1. In developing its Speech Clause jurisprudence, the Supreme Court has created special rules for special settings:

   a. the particularized rules governing speech on public property (the "public forum" doctrine);

b. the Court's "medium-specific" approach to communications media (print, broadcast, cable television, and the Internet);

c. the lesser protection afforded speech in "restricted" environments (schools, prisons, and the military);

d. the limited speech rights of public employees;

e. the Court's special deference to restrictions on government-**funded** expression; and

f. campaign finance law — the regulation of political contributions and expenditures.

2. **Speech on Public Property: the Public Forum Doctrine**

a. Access to public property for speech-related activity is governed by the public forum doctrine.

b. Nothing in the Constitution "requires the Government freely to grant access to all who wish to exercise their right to free speech on every type of Government property without regard to the nature of the property or to the disruption that might be caused by the speaker's activities." ***Cornelius v. NAACP Legal Defense & Education Fund, Inc.,*** 473 U.S. 788, 799-800 (1985).

c. Accordingly, the Supreme Court has adopted a "forum-based" approach to assessing restrictions that the government seeks to place on the use of its property. ***International Society for Krishna Consciousness, Inc. v. Lee,*** 505 U.S. 672, 678 (1992).

d. Government-owned property has been divided into three categories for purposes of forum analysis:

1) "traditional" public forums;

2) "designated" public forums; and

3) "nonpublic" forums, this last category comprising all of the government property not embraced within the first two.

e. Traditional public forums are places that "by long tradition or by government fiat have been devoted to assembly and debate," ***Perry Education Association v. Perry Local Educators' Association,*** 460 U.S. 37, 45 (1983) — including, for example, such areas as public streets, parks, and sidewalks.

f. Designated public forums are places that the government "has opened for expressive activity by part or all of the public," ***Krishna Consciousness,*** 505 U.S. at 678 — including, for example, university meeting facilities and municipal theaters.

g. Nonpublic forums are places that, by tradition, nature, or design, "are not appropriate platforms for unrestrained communication," ***Paulsen v. County of Nassau,*** 925 F.2d 65, 69 (2d Cir. 1991) — including, for example, military installations and federal workplaces.

h. In forum analysis, the government's power to impose speech restrictions depends on how the affected property is categorized; the level of judicial scrutiny hinges on whether the property is deemed a traditional, designated, or nonpublic forum. ***Krishna Consciousness,*** 505 U.S. at 678-79.

i. Traditional public forums may be regulated only via content-neutral time, place, and manner restrictions. To survive judicial scrutiny, such restrictions must be "'justified without reference to the content of the regulated speech,'" must be "'narrowly tailored to serve a significant government interest,'" and must "'leave open ample alternative channels for communication of the information.'" ***Ward v. Rock Against Racism,*** 491 U.S. 781, 791 (1989) (quoting ***Clark v. Community for Creative Non-Violence,*** 468 U.S. 288, 293 (1984)).

j. Governmental restrictions on the **content** of public forum speech are presumptively unconstitutional; they will be struck down unless shown to be "necessary, and narrowly drawn, to serve a compelling state interest." ***Capitol Square Review & Advisory Board v. Pinette,*** 515 U.S. 753, 761 (1995).

k. These same standards govern the second category — restrictions on speech in **designated** public forums. ***Krishna Consciousness,*** 505 U.S. at 678-79. Though the government may limit access to certain speakers (e.g., student groups) or certain subjects (e.g., school board business), and though it need not keep such a forum open indefinitely, its restrictions must be applied evenhandedly to all similarly situated parties. ***Perry,*** 460 U.S. at 45-46 & n.7, 48.

l. Judicial scrutiny is substantially relaxed, however, vis-à-vis the third category — restrictions on speech in **nonpublic** forums. Here, the government enjoys "maximum control over communicative behavior" because its role "is most analogous to that of a private owner." ***Paulsen,*** 925 F.2d at 69.

m. The challenged regulation need only be reasonable, so long as it is not an effort "to suppress expression merely because public officials oppose the speaker's view." ***Perry,*** 460 U.S. at 46.

n. Indeed, control over access to a nonpublic forum can be based on subject matter or speaker identity, "'so long as the distinctions drawn are reasonable in light of the purpose served by the forum and are viewpoint neutral.'" ***United States v. Kokinda,*** 479 U.S. 720, 730 (1990) (quoting ***Cornelius,*** 473 U.S. at 806)).

o. Ultimately, the government's decision to restrict access to a nonpublic forum "need only be reasonable; it need not be the most reasonable or the only reasonable limitation." ***Kokinda,*** 479 U.S. at 730.

p. In distinguishing among these three categories, the Supreme Court has advanced narrow definitions of both traditional and designated public forums.

q. Traditional public forums "are places which 'by long tradition or by government fiat have been devoted to assembly and debate'" — places whose "principal purpose…is the free exchange of ideas." ***Cornelius,*** 473 U.S. at 802 (quoting ***Perry,*** 460 U.S. at 45) & 800.

r. Designated public forums are likewise narrowly conceived. The government does not create such a forum by inaction, or by allowing the public freely to visit, or by permitting limited discourse there; instead, such a forum is created only where the government intentionally opens a nontraditional forum for public discourse. ***Krishna Consciousness,*** 505 U.S. at 680.

s. Under these definitions, public forum status has eluded such heavily frequented public spaces as airport terminals, state fairgrounds, post office sidewalks, public housing complexes, and Chicago's municipally-owned pier.

t. In divining the requisite intent to create a designated public forum, the Court will look to the government's "policy and practice" vis-à-vis the property; it will likewise inquire whether the property is by nature "compatib[le] with expressive activity." ***Cornelius,*** 473 U.S. at 802.

u. As the Court observed in ***Cornelius,*** "We will not find that a public forum has been created in the face of clear evidence of a contrary intent, nor will we infer that the government intended to create a public forum when the nature of the property is inconsistent with expressive activity." 473 U.S. at 803.

v. **Injunctive Restrictions on Public Forum Access and Expression**

1) **Injunctions** that impose content-neutral time, place, or manner restrictions are subject to a heightened form of intermediate scrutiny — under a test that is slightly more stringent than that for legislation.

2) Observing that "[i]njunctions…carry greater risks of censorship and discriminatory application than do general ordinances," the Supreme Court held in 1994 that speech-restrictive injunctions should be subjected by appellate courts to more "stringent" First Amendment scrutiny than comparable legislation — that, "when evaluating a content-neutral **injunction**, we think that our standard time, place, and manner analysis is not sufficiently rigorous." ***Madsen v. Women's Health Center, Inc.,*** 512 U.S. 735, 764-65 (1994) (emphasis added).

3) Announcing a new standard of review for content-neutral **injunctions**, the Court held that, rather than inquiring whether the order is narrowly tailored to serve a significant governmental interest, "[w]e must ask instead whether the challenged provisions of the injunction **burden no more speech than necessary** to serve a significant government interest." *Id.* at 765 (emphasis added).

w. **An Important Exception to the Public Forum Doctrine: The Installation of Permanent Monuments on Public Property**

1) When the government decides to accept or reject a privately donated monument for permanent installation on public property, the public forum doctrine does ***not*** apply.

2) Instead the **"government speech"** doctrine applies, which means that the government's decision is not subject to the Free Speech Clause. ***Pleasant Grove City v. Summum,*** 129 S. Ct. 1125, 1131 (2009).

3) But the government's decision is not wholly free from constitutional restraint. Government speech must comport with the Establishment Clause. 129 S. Ct. at 1131-32.

3. **Restricted Environments: the Military, Prisons, and Schools**

a. In each of these restricted environments, the "inmates" are afforded far less speech protection than their counterparts in the outside world.

b. **The Military:**

1) Recognizing profoundly limited speech protections within the context of military service, the Court in ***Parker v. Levy,*** 417 U.S. 733 (1974) upheld the court martial conviction of an army captain who urged black enlisted men to refuse to fight in Vietnam.

2) Since "'[a]n army is not a deliberative body,'" *id.* at 743-44 (quoting ***In re Grimley,*** 137 U.S. 147, 153 (1890)), and since obedience to lawful commands is essential to the effective functioning of military units, *id.* at 758, the type of **dis**obedience urged here by the defendant finds **no** First Amendment protection.

3) Citing a commander's need to maintain morale, discipline, and readiness, the Court in ***Brown v. Glines,*** 444 U.S. 348, 356 (1980) went far beyond ***Parker,*** upholding a regulation that required service members to obtain advance permission from their commander before circulating any petition on an Air Force base.

c. **Prisons:**

1) In ***Jones v. North Carolina Prisoners' Union,*** 433 U.S. 119 (1977), the Court upheld direct restrictions on efforts by prison inmates to form and operate a union — including a ban on soliciting other inmates to join the union, meetings among union members, and bulk mailings concerning the union from outside sources.

2) Delivering the opinion of the Court, Justice Rehnquist established an extremely deferential standard for gauging restrictions on inmate speech.

3) Recognizing "the wide-ranging deference to be accorded the decisions of prison administrators," *id.* at 126, Rehnquist asserted that "'in the absence of substantial evidence in the record to indicate that the officials have exaggerated their response to [security] considerations, courts should ordinarily defer to their expert judgment in such matters,'" *id.* at 128 (quoting ***Pell v. Procunier,*** 417 U.S. 817, 827 (1974)).

4) Ten years later, in ***Turner v. Safley,*** 482 U.S. 78 (1987), the Court upheld broad restrictions on inmate-to-inmate correspondence — and, in the process, reaffirmed its commitment to a deferential standard in prisoner speech cases.

5) Announcing a test that prevails to this day, Justice O'Connor held that "when a prison regulation impinges on inmates' constitutional rights, the regulation is valid if it is **reasonably related to legitimate penological interests**." *Id.* at 89.

6) Justice O'Connor's opinion in ***Turner*** identified four factors to consider when applying this standard (*id.* at 89-91):

   a) whether there exists a valid, rational connection between the regulation and the governmental interest put forward to justify it;

   b) whether inmates are left with alternative means of exercising the right that the regulation restricts;

   c) whether accommodating the asserted right would have a significant ripple effect on fellow inmates or prison staff; and

   d) whether there is a ready alternative to the regulation that fully accommodates the asserted right at a **de minimis** cost to valid penological interests.

d. **Schools:**

1) Students in public secondary schools do not enjoy the same highly-protected speech rights as do their adult counterparts in the outside world. Protection for student speech will vary depending upon which of the following four categories it falls into:

a) **Individual Political Expression:** This is the type of student speech that receives the greatest protection. It may only be censored or punished by school authorities if it **"materially and substantially disrupt[s]"** the work and discipline of the school. ***Tinker v. Des Moines School District***, 393 U.S. 503, 509 (1969) (holding that school officials violated the First Amendment rights of students by banning them from wearing, and then suspending them for wearing, black armbands as a symbol of opposition to the Vietnam War). NOTE: This **substantial disruption** test is the most speech-protective test in the realm of student expression — and it DOES NOT APPLY in any of the other categories of student speech.

b) **Lewd or Vulgar Speech:** Student speech that is lewd or vulgar may be readily censored or punished by school authorities. ***Bethel School District No. 403 v. Fraser***, 478 U.S. 675 (1986) (upholding disciplinary action in which a student was punished for delivering a sophomoric, sexually suggestive speech at a high school assembly). The speech, made in support of a candidate for student government, contained an elaborate sexual metaphor: "Jeff Kuhlman is a man who takes his point and pounds it in….He doesn't attack things in spurts. He drives hard, pushing and pushing until finally — he succeeds." 478 U.S. at 687.

c) **Speech Advocating or Celebrating Illegal Drug Use:** Student speech that advocates or celebrates illegal drug use may be readily censored or punished by school authorities. ***Morse v. Frederick***, 127 S. Ct. 2618 (2007) (upholding suspension of student who unfurled a 14-foot-long banner — bearing the phrase "BONG HiTS 4 JESUS" — while standing in front of his school with classmates and administrators as the televised procession of the Olympic Torch Relay passed before them). Rejecting the argument that this banner was a form of political speech protected by ***Tinker***, the Supreme Court held that "a principal may, consistent with the First Amendment, restrict student speech at a school event, when that speech is reasonably viewed as promoting illegal drug use." 127 S. Ct. at 2625.

d) **School-Sponsored Speech:** Efforts by school officials to edit, restrict, or censor student speech that appears in an official school publication or otherwise bears the school's "imprimatur" will be analyzed by courts under a form of **rational basis** review — the speech restriction will be upheld if it is "reasonably related to legitimate pedagogical concerns." ***Hazelwood School District v. Kuhlmeier***, 484 U.S. 260, 272-73 (1988) (upholding a high school principal's decision to remove two articles from the student newspaper — a story describing three students' experiences with pregnancy, and a story discussing the impact of divorce on students at the school). NOTE: This category is confined to student speech that appears in a publication or setting that may be reasonably perceived to bear the school's stamp of approval.

2) The ***Bethel*** decision is limited to **lewd** and **vulgar** speech — its deferential treatment of school censorship does NOT extend to speech that is deemed **"offensive"** by administrators. ***Morse v. Frederick***, 127 S. Ct. 2618, 2629 (2007). This holding repudiates a longstanding trend in the lower federal courts.

3) Flatly rejecting the arguments of the Bush Administration, and repudiating yet another trend in the lower federal courts, ***Morse v. Frederick*** refused to hold that the First Amendment permits public school officials to censor any student speech that purportedly interferes with a school's "educational mission." 127 S. Ct. at 2637 (Alito and Kennedy, JJ., concurring).

4. **Speech Rights of Public Employees**

a. The Supreme Court has created special rules governing the speech rights of public employees.

b. These rules essentially balance a government employer's interest in promoting workplace efficiency against the employee's interest in commenting freely on matters of public concern.

Watch Out!

This line of cases will protect the public employee only if she was speaking as a CITIZEN and not in her official capacity as a government worker. ***Garcetti v. Ceballos,*** 547 U.S. 410 (2006). Thus, if you get a fact pattern in which a public employee is being punished by her government employer for something she said or wrote, look carefully at the ***context*** in which she made the statement and ask yourself: "When the employee made that statement, was she acting pursuant to her official duties or was she speaking as a citizen?" Only in the latter situation does the First Amendment apply.

c. When an employee criticizes her government employer, the difficulty in these cases is to determine whether her words are protected political speech or an unprotected act of insubordination.

d. This dichotomy is exemplified in two Supreme Court cases:

1) ***Pickering v. Board of Education,*** 391 U.S. 563 (1968); and

2) ***Connick v. Myers,*** 461 U.S. 138 (1983).

e. In ***Pickering,*** a public schoolteacher had been fired for a letter he had published in a local newspaper criticizing the school board's spending of tax revenues and questioning its purported need for new revenues.

f. In ***Connick,*** an assistant district attorney had been fired for circulating a workplace questionnaire inquiring whether her colleagues felt pressured to work in political campaigns in order to keep their jobs.

g. The Court sided with the schoolteacher in ***Pickering***, holding that school tax levies are matters of legitimate public concern and that teachers should "be able to speak out freely on such questions without fear of retaliatory dismissal." 391 U.S. at 571-72.

h. But in ***Connick***, the Court sided with the employer, who described the questionnaire as an act of insubordination that prompted a "mini-insurrection" in the workplace. 461 U.S. at 151.

   1) The Court concluded that the questionnaire "touched upon matters of public concern in only the most limited sense," and was therefore worthy of only minimal First Amendment protection. *Id.* at 154.

   2) Thus, the balance of interests favored the employer, who was not required to "tolerate action which he reasonably believed would disrupt the office, undermine his authority, and destroy close working relationships." *Id.* at 154.

i. ***Connick*** shows that speech by a public employee will be afforded ever greater weight in this balancing analysis the more it ascends from a personal workplace grievance to pure political expression.

j. Thus, in ***Rankin v. McPherson,*** 483 U.S. 378 (1987), the Court sided with a clerical worker in a county constable's office who had been fired for expressing her contempt for the policies of President Reagan.

   1) Apprised of the assassination attempt on Reagan, the plaintiff cited his cutbacks on welfare, food stamps, and medicaid, and declared: "[I]f they go for him again, I hope they get him." *Id.* at 381.

   2) This statement, held the Court, was plainly a form of political expression, since it was uttered in the context of a conversation criticizing Reagan's policies. *Id.* at 386.

   3) And the "inappropriate or controversial character" of the statement was "irrelevant" to whether it dealt with a matter of public concern. *Id.* at 387.

   4) Applying its balancing test to these facts, the Court concluded that the speech rights of the employee trumped the employer's interests, since there was no proof that her statement, uttered in a private conversation, either discredited the office or interfered with its efficient operation. *Id.* at 389.

k. SUMMING UP THE ANALYSIS TO PERFORM IN PUBLIC EMPLOYEE SPEECH CASES: Under the First Amendment, a public employer may not retaliate against a public employee for engaging in protected speech. Under the ***Connick-Pickering*** test, a public employee can establish that her speech is constitutionally protected if (1) the employee spoke as a citizen on matters of public concern; and (2) the interest of the employee as a citizen in commenting upon matters of public concern outweighs the interest of the State as an employer in promoting the efficiency of the public services it performs through its employees. When applying Prong #1 of that test, remember the holding in ***Garcetti***: "[W]hen public employees make statements pursuant to their official duties, the employees are not speaking as citizens for First Amendment purposes, and the Constitution does not insulate their communications from employer discipline." 547 U.S. at 421. When applying the balancing test in Prong #2, the primary question is whether the employee's speech has undermined "the effective functioning of the public employer's enterprise." ***Rankin v. McPherson***, 483 U.S. 378, 388 (1987). In order to win her case, the public employee must prevail on both prongs of the ***Connick-Pickering*** test.

l. In related lines of precedent, the Court has held that government workers are constitutionally protected from dismissal for refusing to take an oath regarding their political affiliation. ***Keyishian v. Board of Regents,*** 385 U.S. 589 (1967); ***Elfbrandt v. Russell,*** 384 U.S. 11 (1966); ***Wieman v. Updegraff,*** 344 U.S. 183 (1952).

m. Likewise, except where relevant to job performance, it is unconstitutional to discharge a government worker or deny her a promotion based on her affiliation with a particular political party.

1) Discharge: ***Branti v. Finkel,*** 445 U.S. 507 (1980); ***Elrod v. Burns,*** 427 U.S. 347 (1976). These protections against patronage discharge were extended to independent contractors in ***O'Hare Truck Service, Inc. v. City of Northlake,*** 518 U.S. 712 (1996).

2) Promotion Denial: ***Rutan v. Republican Party of Illinois,*** 497 U.S. 62 (1990).

5. **Government-Funded Expression**

a. In this special context — where the government is **funding** expressive activity -- the Supreme Court's review is utterly deferential, upholding even **viewpoint** discrimination.

b. In ***Rust v. Sullivan,*** 500 U.S. 173 (1991), for example, the Court held that Congress does not offend the First Amendment by making federal public health funding conditioned upon the recipient's abstaining from providing counseling about abortion or advocating abortion as a method of family planning.

b. ***Rust's*** upshot was to broaden the government's power to exert control over the speech of government grantees — permitting **viewpoint** discrimination in doling out government subsidies.

c. The Court upheld a federal statute imposing viewpoint-based discrimination in public arts funding. ***National Endowment for the Arts v. Finley,*** 524 U.S. 569, 606 (1998) (Souter, J., dissenting) (citing the statute's "decency and respect proviso," which required that funding applications be judged "'under general standards of decency and respect for the diverse beliefs and values of the American public,'" as a patent example of "viewpoint discrimination").

d. In its latest speech funding case, the Supreme Court demonstrated once again that when the government is ***subsidizing*** speech, it has much greater power to control the content of that speech. ***United States v. American Library Association***, 539 U.S. 194 (2003) (rejecting a free speech challenge to a federal funding program that required public libraries to use Internet filters as a condition for receipt of federal subsidies).

6. **Campaign Finance Law — the Regulation of Political Contributions and Expenditures**.

a. For many years, the dominant Supreme Court case in this area has been ***Buckley v. Valeo***, 424 U.S. 1 (1976). ***Buckley*** drew a distinction between:

(1) CONTRIBUTIONS TO a candidate, and

(2) EXPENDITURES BY or FOR a candidate.

b. ***Buckley*** held that CONTRIBUTIONS to a candidate may be limited, but EXPENDITURES by or for a candidate may ***not***, except as a condition of receiving public funds.

c. In ***Citizens United v. Federal Election Commission,*** 130 S. Ct. 876 (2010), the Supreme Court reaffirmed ***Buckley*** and greatly simplified the law of campaign finance.

d. ***Citizens United*** retains ***Buckley's*** distinction between DIRECT CONTRIBUTIONS to a candidate (which ***can*** be restricted) and INDEPENDENT EXPENDITURES FOR a candidate (which now ***cannot*** be restricted).

e. As to these INDEPENDENT EXPENDITURES, ***Citizens United*** holds that:

1) Congress cannot impose ***dollar limits*** on them;

2) Congress cannot bar ***corporations*** from making them, even if the corporation is spending the money to disseminate a partisan political message; and

3) Congress cannot restrict their ***timing*** (banning them, for example, in the final days leading up to an election).

f. But independent expenditures in the form of corporate political speech CAN be regulated through DISCLAIMER and DISCLOSURE requirements that reveal the identity of the speaker.

III. FREEDOM OF THE PRESS

A. A "PREFERRED" STATUS FOR THE PRESS?

1. Does the press enjoy a "preferred" status under the First Amendment? The short answer is an emphatic "NO."

2. Indeed, the Press Clause is itself surprisingly irrelevant. The landmark cases in which press freedom has been vindicated (e.g., the Pentagon Papers case) were decided under the SPEECH Clause, NOT the Press Clause.

3. Ironically, liberty of the PRESS received much more attention than liberty of speech among 18th century advocates of expressive freedom.

4. In a 1975 law review article, Justice Stewart argued that the Press Clause is **redundant** if it offers no protection beyond that afforded by the Speech Clause — and the Framers CANNOT have intended such a result.

   a. Stewart asserted that the Framers envisioned the Press Clause as providing an ADDITIONAL structural check on the three branches of government by protecting the institutional autonomy of The Fourth Estate.

   b. But three years later, in ***First National Bank of Boston v. Bellotti,*** 435 U.S. 765, 797-801 (1978), Chief Justice Burger, in a concurrence that reflects the longstanding majority view, rejected Stewart's "special-protection-for-the-press" argument.

   c. The Supreme Court has consistently refused to hold that the press enjoys any special protection from the enforcement of generally applicable laws.

B. A RIGHT TO "GATHER" NEWS?

1. The following cases show that:

   a. the press enjoys no special power or privilege to gather information;

   b. the press enjoys no greater right of access to government information or proceedings than that enjoyed by the general public; and

c. the press enjoys no special immunity from governmental demands for information in its possession.

2. ***Branzburg v. Hayes,*** 408 U.S. 665 (1972): In an opinion widely regarded as **rejecting** any special Press Clause protection for news-gathering by the media, the Supreme Court holds that there is no reporter/news source privilege, so that reporters can be compelled to disclose their investigative findings and the identities of their sources when subpoenaed to testify before grand juries.

   a. In ***Branzburg***, a reporter was subpoenaed to reveal the identities of confidential news sources for a series of articles he had written on illegal drug activity.

   b. In a dissent joined by Brennan and Marshall, Justice Stewart asserted: By leaving reporters with no privilege by which to protect their sources, the majority opinion invites law enforcement officials to turn the "independent" press into an investigative arm of the government.

3. In ***Branzburg's*** wake, a majority of states have enacted "shield" laws designed to protect the confidentiality of press sources.

   a. But these shield laws are largely toothless.

   b. Reporters still go to **jail** (usually for contempt of court) rather than reveal their sources.

4. ***Zurcher v. Stanford Daily,*** 436 U.S. 547 (1978) upheld the newsroom search of a college paper's editorial offices, holding that so long as the search satisfies the Fourth Amendment, the First Amendment affords the news media no special protection from search and seizure.

   a. In ***Zurcher***, a student newspaper published articles and photographs concerning a violent clash on campus between demonstrators and police. Seeking negatives and photos that might help them identify those demonstrators, police obtained a warrant and searched the paper's editorial offices, where they rifled the filing cabinets, desks, wastepaper baskets, and photographic laboratories.

   b. The Court, in an opinion by Justice White, rejected the newspaper's civil action against the police.

   c. Justice Stewart, dissenting in ***Zurcher***, warned that a search warrant directed at a newspaper permits the "ransacking" of the paper's files.

   d. In ***Zurcher's*** wake, Congress enacted the Privacy Protection Act of 1980.

   e. The Act limits the power of law enforcement officials to conduct newsroom searches, unless the media target is itself suspected of criminal wrongdoing or there are reasonable grounds to believe that the evidence would be destroyed if sought by subpoena rather than a warrant.

f. Notwithstanding the Act, ***Zurcher*** still shows that the Press Clause affords the news media no greater protection from search and seizure than that enjoyed by the public generally.

5. Likewise, ***Pell v. Procunier,*** 417 U.S. 817 (1974) and ***Houchins v. KQED,*** 438 U.S. 1 (1978) show that reporters enjoy no greater access to jails than that enjoyed by the public generally.

   a. ***Pell*** upheld a California penal provision barring face-to-face interviews between inmates and reporters.

   b. ***KQED*** — confirming that the press enjoys no special right of access to news sources and information under government control — upheld a penal provision restricting press and public access to a particular wing of a jail.

5. Press Access to Governmental Information and Proceedings: ***Richmond Newspapers*** and Its Progeny

   a. In ***Richmond Newspapers v. Virginia,*** 448 U.S. 555 (1980), the Supreme Court recognized a general right of public and press access to criminal trials. But this right is NOT a special Press Clause right enjoyed by the news media; it is a general First Amendment right of PUBLIC ACCESS.

   b. Invoking the Speech, Press, Assembly, and Petition Clauses of the First Amendment, ***Richmond Newspapers*** asserted that "[t]hese expressly guaranteed freedoms share a common core purpose of assuring freedom of communication on matters relating to the **functioning of government**." 448 U.S. at 575 (emphasis added).

   c. Thus, the First Amendment confers upon the public a broad "right to know" about governmental proceedings: "[T]he First Amendment goes beyond protection of the press and the self-expression of individuals to prohibit government from limiting the stock of information from which members of the public may draw. Free speech carries with it some freedom to listen. In a variety of contexts, this Court has referred to a First Amendment right to receive information and ideas." *Id.* at 575-76 (citations and internal quotations omitted).

   d. "People in an open society," said the Court, "do not demand infallibility from their institutions, but it is difficult for them to accept what they are prohibited from observing." *Id.* at 572.

   e. Based, then, on this broad "right to know," the Court has issued a series of decisions guaranteeing public access to criminal proceedings:

1) ***Richmond Newspapers,*** 448 U.S. at 580 (holding that "the right to attend criminal trials is implicit in the guarantees of the First Amendment");

2) ***Globe Newspaper Co. v. Superior Court for the County of Norfolk,*** 457 U.S. 596 (1982) (striking down restrictions on public access to rape trials);

3) ***Press-Enterprise Co. v. Superior Court of California (Press-Enterprise I),*** 464 U.S. 501 (1984) (guaranteeing public access to voir dire examinations in criminal proceedings); and

4) ***Press-Enterprise Co. v. Superior Court of California (Press-Enterprise II),*** 478 U.S. 1 (1986) (recognizing a qualified First Amendment right of public access to preliminary hearings in criminal trials conducted in California).

f. In deciding whether the First Amendment confers a right of public access to certain governmental proceedings, the Supreme Court has examined "two complementary considerations," ***Press-Enterprise II,*** 478 U.S. at 8:

1) whether the proceedings "have historically been open to the press and general public," and

2) "whether public access plays a significant positive role in the functioning of the particular process in question."

g. If, based on this analysis, the public DOES enjoy a right of access, any governmental restriction on such access will be gauged under **strict scrutiny**.

h. Ultimately, though, the PRESS enjoys only that degree of access enjoyed by the public generally — and such access is by no means derived specifically from the PRESS Clause. It is derived instead from the PUBLIC's "right to know" — a right first recognized in ***Richmond Newspapers*** as emanating from the Speech, Press, Assembly, and Petition Clauses in combination.

C. DIFFERENTIAL TREATMENT OF THE PRESS

1. Where the government SINGLES OUT the press for special burdens, the Supreme Court will employ strict scrutiny.

2. **See, e.g.,** ***Minneapolis Star & Tribune Co. v. Minnesota Commissioner of Revenue,*** 460 U.S. 575 (1983): striking down a special tax on paper and ink employed in the publishing of periodicals.

   a. Writing for the Court, Justice O'Connor observed that differential taxation of the press would have troubled the Framers.

D. REGULATING THE PRESS TO "IMPROVE" THE MARKETPLACE OF IDEAS

1. We have already seen — in the context of "indecency" — that the Supreme Court's approach to mass communications media is to analyze each medium according to its unique history and characteristics.

    a. At the top of the totem pole, receiving unqualified protection, are the print medium (***Miami Herald***) and cyberspace (***Reno v. ACLU***).

    b. At the bottom of the totem pole, subject to the greatest degree of content-based regulation, is the broadcast medium (***Pacifica*** and ***Red Lion***).

    c. Adrift in an undecided no man's land is the medium of cable TV. ***Denver Area Educational Telecommunications Consortium, Inc. v. FCC,*** 518 U.S. 727, 739-43 (1996) (the four-justice plurality opinion leaves open the possibility that a lesser First Amendment standard, comparable to that reserved for broadcasting, might apply to cable TV).

2. In accordance with this "totem pole" approach, the Court has protected the print medium, but has **not** protected the broadcast and cable media, from government regulations that amounted to compelled speech:

    a. ***Turner Broadcasting System, Inc. v. FCC*** (***Turner I***), 512 U.S. 622 (1994) & ***Turner Broadcasting System, Inc. v. FCC*** (***Turner II***), 520 U.S. 180 (1997) (upholding "must carry" provisions for cable TV);

    b. ***Columbia Broadcasting System v. FCC,*** 453 U.S. 367 (1981) (upholding an FCC rule requiring broadcasters to "allow reasonable access [by] a legally qualified candidate for Federal elective office on behalf of his candidacy");

    c. ***Miami Herald Publishing Co. v. Tornillo,*** 418 U.S. 241 (1974) (invalidating a "right of reply" statute requiring any newspaper that "assails" the character of a political candidate to print the candidate's reply);

    d. ***Red Lion Broadcasting Co. v. FCC,*** 395 U.S. 367 (1969) (upholding the FCC's "fairness doctrine," which imposed on **broadcasters** precisely the sort of "right of reply" provision that the Court later rejected for the PRINT medium in **Miami Herald**).

        1) Though the FCC has now repealed the "fairness doctrine," do not conclude from this that any change has occurred in CONSTITUTIONAL law.

        2) Merely because the government has CHOSEN not to regulate does not mean that the Press Clause has expanded overnight.

3) Even if it CHOOSES not to do so, the government has the POWER to reenact the fairness doctrine tomorrow — and broadcasters have no Press Clause protection against its renewed enforcement.

IV. FREEDOM OF ASSOCIATION

A. INTRODUCTION TO FREEDOM OF ASSOCIATION

1. The First Amendment does not mention "freedom of association," but the Supreme Court has inferred the existence of such a right as a necessary concomitant to the express protections for speech, assembly, and petition.

2. Freedom of association protects a person's right to join together with others for the purpose of pursuing social, political, or economic goals.

3. Freedom of association is implicated in six scattered lines of First Amendment precedent:

   a. An organization's freedom from compelled disclosure of its members

   b. A speaker's freedom from compelled disclosure of her identity

   c. A person's freedom from punishment based on her political associations or opinions

   d. A person's freedom from compelled membership in an organization

   e. An organization's freedom from compelled inclusion of unwanted members

   f. Litigation as an associational right

B. AN ORGANIZATION'S FREEDOM FROM COMPELLED DISCLOSURE OF ITS MEMBERS

1. Freedom of association was first recognized by the Supreme Court in a line of cases protecting unpopular organizations from the compelled disclosure of their membership lists.

2. The most famous of these cases is ***NAACP v. Alabama,*** 357 U.S. 449 (1958).

   a. Striking down enforcement of Alabama's corporate "doing-business" statute, by which the government sought to compel disclosure of the NAACP's membership list.

   b. This enforcement was part of an effort by government officials to oust the NAACP from the State of Alabama.

c. The NAACP produced substantially all of the records called for — **except** its membership list, prompting a state court's contempt order and a fine of $100,000.

d. Justice Harlan, writing for the Court, likened this type of compelled disclosure to "'[a] requirement that adherents of particular religious faiths or political parties wear identifying armbands.'" 357 U.S. at 462 (quoting ***American Communications Association v. Douds,*** 339 U.S. 382, 402 (1950)).

e. Especially where a group espouses **dissident** views, there is a strong likelihood that compelled disclosure of affiliation with that group will chill the freedom of association — since revealing a member's identity exposes him to the threat of **reprisal**. *Id.* at 462.

f. As Harlan pointed out, revelation of NAACP membership had previously exposed its rank-and-file members to "economic reprisal, loss of employment, threat of physical coercion, and other manifestations of public hostility."

g. Applying strict scrutiny, Harlan concluded that Alabama's justification for demanding disclosure of the membership list — to determine whether the NAACP was conducting intrastate business — was hardly sufficient to satisfy the requisite "compelling interest" test.

C. A SPEAKER'S FREEDOM FROM COMPELLED DISCLOSURE OF HER IDENTITY

1. Harlan's insight — that the protective cloak of anonymity helps to preserve the First Amendment freedoms of political minorities — proved pivotal in ***McIntyre v. Ohio Elections Commission,*** 514 U.S. 334 (1995) and ***Talley v. California,*** 362 U.S. 60 (1960), where the Supreme Court struck down bans on anonymous leafleting.

2. In ***Talley,*** which involved the distribution of unsigned handbills urging readers to boycott certain Los Angeles merchants for engaging in discriminatory employment practices, Justice Black, writing for the Court, observed that "[p]ersecuted groups and sects from time to time throughout history have been able to criticize oppressive practices and laws either anonymously or not at all." 362 U.S. at 64.

   a. Black stressed that "[a]nonymous pamphlets, leaflets, brochures and even books have played an important role in the progress of mankind." *Id.* at 64.

   b. He cited the experience of American colonists, who "frequently had to conceal their authorship or distribution of literature that easily could have brought down on them prosecutions by English-controlled courts." *Id.* at 65.

   c. "Even the Federalist Papers, written in favor of the adoption of our Constitution, were published under fictitious names." *Id.* at 65.

d. "It is plain," he concluded, "that anonymity has sometimes been assumed for the most constructive purposes." *Id.* at 65.

3. Writing for the Court in ***McIntyre***, where a 7-2 majority struck down Ohio's ban on anonymous campaign literature, Justice Stevens surveyed the broad range of literary and political authors who chose to publish anonymously or under pseudonyms — including Mark Twain, Voltaire, George Sand, George Eliot, Charles Dickens, and, during the period surrounding our Revolution and Founding, "Publius," "Junius," "Cato," "Centinel," and "The Federal Farmer." 514 U.S. at 341-43.

4. Stevens concluded: "Under our Constitution, anonymous pamphleteering is not a pernicious, fraudulent practice, but an honorable tradition of advocacy and dissent. Anonymity is a shield from the tyranny of the majority. It thus exemplifies the purpose behind the Bill of Rights, and of the First Amendment in particular: to protect unpopular individuals from retaliation — and their ideas from suppression — at the hand of an intolerant society." 514 U.S. at 357 (citations omitted).

D. A PERSON'S FREEDOM FROM PUNISHMENT BASED ON HER POLITICAL ASSOCIATIONS OR OPINIONS

1. In related lines of precedent, the Court has held that government workers are constitutionally protected from dismissal for refusing to take an oath regarding their political affiliation. ***Keyishian v. Board of Regents,*** 385 U.S. 589 (1967); ***Elfbrandt v. Russell,*** 384 U.S. 11 (1966); ***Wieman v. Updegraff,*** 344 U.S. 183 (1952).

2. Likewise, except where relevant to job performance, it is unconstitutional to discharge a government worker or deny her a promotion based on her affiliation with a particular political party.

   a. Discharge: ***Branti v. Finkel,*** 445 U.S. 507 (1980); ***Elrod v. Burns,*** 427 U.S. 347 (1976). These protections against patronage discharge were extended to independent contractors in ***O'Hare Truck Service, Inc. v. City of Northlake,*** 518 U.S. 712 (1996).

   b. Promotion Denial: ***Rutan v. Republican Party of Illinois,*** 497 U.S. 62 (1990).

E. A PERSON'S FREEDOM FROM COMPELLED MEMBERSHIP IN AN ORGANIZATION

1. The leading case here is ***Abood v. Detroit Board of Education,*** 431 U.S. 209 (1977), which involved compelled payment of union dues by non-union members.

2. Specifically, ***Abood*** involved a challenge to a Michigan statute permitting "agency shop" arrangements in connection with union representation of government employees.

3. The suit was brought by ***non***-union teachers whose employment by the Detroit public school system automatically caused them to be represented by the teachers union.

4. These non-union teachers objected — on First Amendment compelled association grounds — to the agency shop arrangement, under which they were compelled to pay the union a service charge equal in amount to union dues.

5. Since the non-union teachers benefited from the union's **collective bargaining** representation, the Supreme Court held that they could **not** (as "free riders") evade paying for it.

6. But the Court held that they did NOT have to pay for the POLITICAL activities and endorsements in which the union engaged. To make them pay for ideological causes that they found repugnant would violate their First Amendment freedom from compelled speech and association. The union would have to raise money **separately** for such causes.

F. AN ORGANIZATION'S FREEDOM FROM COMPELLED INCLUSION OF UNWANTED MEMBERS

1. **Excluding Women from Civic or Commercial Organizations**

    a. ***Roberts v. United States Jaycees,*** 468 U.S. 609 (1984) (rejecting an effort by the Jaycees to exclude women from their voting membership).

    b. ***Board of Directors of Rotary International v. Rotary Club of Duarte,*** 481 U.S. 537 (1987) (unanimously upholding the application of California's gender discrimination law to the Duarte Rotary Club, a civic organization that refused to admit women).

2. **Barring Gays from the Boy Scouts**

    a. ***Boy Scouts of America v. Dale,*** 530 U.S. 640 (2000) (voting 5-4) (per Rehnquist, C.J.) (holding that the Boy Scouts can ban gay members because opposition to homosexuality is part of the organization's expressive message) (treating the organization as a "public accommodation" such that it was subject to New Jersey's anti-discrimination law violated the Boy Scouts' right to freedom of association, held the Court).

Watch Out!

Do NOT interpret the ***Boy Scouts*** case as a broad authorization for other organizations to exclude gays and lesbians.

To accomplish that outcome in the ***Boy Scouts*** case, Chief Justice Rehnquist had to find that opposition to homosexuality was part of the organization's expressive message. That finding was a stretch even with the ***Boy Scouts***; it won't be possible with most other organizations.

3. **Protecting the Freedom of Political Association in the Context of Primary Election Ballots**

   a. ***California Democratic Party v. Jones,*** 530 U.S. 567 (2000) (voting 7-2) (per Scalia, J.) (striking down California's blanket primary system, under which all voters were given a single ballot from which they could choose candidates of any party affiliation) (holding that this system stripped parties of their right to political association).

4. **Protecting "Expressive Association" in the Context of Marches and Parades**

   a. The leading case here is ***Hurley v. Irish-American Gay, Lesbian & Bisexual Group of Boston,*** 515 U.S. 557 (1995).

      1) Holding that Massachusetts could not invoke its public accommodations law to force the private organizers of a St. Patrick's Day parade to include a contingent of Irish gays and lesbians who would march under a distinct banner and convey a message that the organizers did not wish to impart.

      2) Compelling the inclusion of this group effectively altered the expressive content of the organizers' parade — a type of compelled speech and association that violates the First Amendment.

G. LITIGATION AS AN ASSOCIATIONAL RIGHT

1. The leading case here is ***NAACP v. Button,*** 371 U.S. 415 (1963).

2. Virginia sought to discourage desegregation litigation by the NAACP through enforcement of a statute that proscribed "improper solicitation" of business.

3. The State employed this statute to prohibit the NAACP's practice of explaining to parents and children how to bring a school desegregation suit and distributing forms authorizing the NAACP to represent the signer in such a suit.

4. The Supreme Court held that the NAACP's actions were "modes of expression and association" protected by the First Amendment.

V. THE RELIGION CLAUSES

A. INTRODUCTION TO THE RELIGION CLAUSES

1. In the text of the First Amendment, the Speech and Press Clauses are **preceded** by the two Religion Clauses (the Establishment and Free Exercise Clauses):

"Congress shall make no law respecting an establishment of religion, or prohibiting the free exercise thereof…"

2. Determining **Whether** the Religion Clauses Apply — and, if so, **Which One**

   a. Any factual scenario that features a government/religion nexus arguably implicates the Religion Clauses.

   b. If the scenario involves government aid to, or identification with, religion, the Establishment Clause may apply.

   c. If the scenario involves governmental interference with, or hindrance of, religion, the Free Exercise Clause may apply.

B. THE ESTABLISHMENT CLAUSE

1. For many years, the 3-pronged test from ***Lemon v. Kurtzman,*** 403 U.S. 602 (1971) was the basic standard for gauging Establishment Clause violations.

2. To survive judicial scrutiny under ***Lemon***, a state action:

   a. **must** have a secular purpose (the PURPOSE prong);

   b. **must** have a primary effect that neither advances nor inhibits religion (the EFFECT prong); and

   c. may **not** foster an excessive governmental entanglement with religion (the ENTANGLEMENT prong).

3. Recent and Influential Glosses on the ***Lemon*** Test

   a. Before announcing her retirement from the bench on July 1, 2005, Justice Sandra Day O'Connor had exerted an enormous influence on Establishment Clause jurisprudence. Time will tell whether the Court will some day reject the doctrine that she developed. But your responsibility is to know the law that exists ***today*** — and that law continues to reflect her influence.

   b. Justice O'Connor's "endorsement" approach to Establishment Clause analysis effected a **change** in the application of the ***Lemon*** test — and is worth bearing in mind when **you** apply ***Lemon***.

   c. Based on her influential concurrence in ***Lynch v. Donnelly,*** 465 U.S. 668 (1984) and her majority opinion in ***Agostini v. Felton,*** 521 U.S. 203 (1997), you may safely impose the following glosses on ***Lemon***:

1) The purpose prong of ***Lemon*** inquires whether the government **actually intends** to endorse religion.

2) The effect prong of ***Lemon*** asks whether the challenged practice in fact **conveys** a **message** of government endorsement of religion.

3) In ***Agostini***, the Court began the process of **collapsing** the entanglement prong INTO the effect prong. Writing for the Court in ***Agostini***, O'Connor asserted that the question of entanglement is best treated "[as] an aspect of the inquiry into a statute's effect."

d. ***Zelman v. Simmons-Harris***, 536 U.S. 639 (2002) completed the conversion from ***Lemon's*** three-prong test to ***Agostini's*** two-prong test. Chief Justice Rehnquist's majority opinion does not even mention ***Lemon***; instead, he employs the two-prong purpose/effect standard from ***Agostini***. In her concurrence, Justice O'Connor does cite ***Lemon***, but she confirms that it has now been modified into the two-prong inquiry performed in ***Agostini***.

Essay Advice

For states that also test Constitutional Law in essay form

Since bar examiners may be slow to recognize this change, our advice is this: **In answering any essay question** that presents an Establishment Clause issue, begin by laying out the original three-prong ***Lemon*** test, and then explain how, in the wake of ***Agostini*** and ***Zelman***, the prevailing standard is now a two-prong purpose/effect test.

MBE Advice

On the Multistate, any reference to ***Lemon*** is not per se incorrect, since the case has not been overruled – but, given the choice, you should prefer ***Agostini's*** two-prong test to ***Lemon's*** now-outdated three-prong standard.

4. **Recommended Analysis**

a. Taken as a whole, the Court's Establishment Clause cases are very difficult to reconcile. But the task becomes easier if you break the cases down into three distinct lines of precedent. Reduced to the following three scenarios, the Court's decisions (or at least the **results** in those cases) become more coherent:

> ***Establishment Clause cases — 3 scenarios:***
>
> ***Category 1:*** Government **aid** to religious institutions
>
> ***Category 2:*** Government **identification** with religion
>
> ***Category 3:*** Religious **teachings** or **practices** within a governmental ceremony or institution

1) Government **aid** to religious institutions (whether in the form of a subsidy or service) —

   e.g., ***Mitchell v. Helms,*** 530 U.S. 793 (2000) (rejecting an Establishment Clause challenge to a federal program that places computers in the classrooms of public and parochial schools alike).

2) Government **identification** with religion (often featuring religious **symbols** erected on, in, or near a government building) —

   e.g., ***Lynch v. Donnelly,*** 465 U.S. 668 (1984) (rejecting an Establishment Clause challenge to a municipal Christmas display that featured a crèche surrounded by a large number of secular elements, including a Santa Claus house, reindeer, candy-striped poles, and a sign that read "Season's Greetings").

3) Religious **teachings** or **practices** within a governmental ceremony or institution —

   e.g., ***Santa Fe Independent School District v. Doe,*** 530 U.S. 290 (2000) (striking down a public high school policy permitting student-led, student-initiated prayers prior to football games).

b. As for Category #1 (government **aid** to religious institutions), the Court will likely uphold such aid so long as it is available **across the board**, to secular and sectarian institutions **alike**. Moreover, the Court will uphold across-the-board aid even when religious institutions end up receiving a disproportionate share of it — if the disparity results from the "private choice" of parents to send their children (the ultimate targets of the aid) to religious schools. (This "private choice" theme is discussed more fully below.)

c. As for Category #2 (government **identification** with religion, often featuring religious **symbols** erected on, in, or near a government building), such displays are likely to survive judicial scrutiny only if they incorporate **secular** elements.

d. As for Category #3 (religious **teachings** or **practices** within a governmental ceremony or institution), this is where the Court is most hostile and most willing to find an Establishment Clause violation. It is here where the state action most arguably crosses the line from "endorsement" to "coercion," and thus becomes far more vulnerable to challenge.

e. One additional factor to bear in mind when performing an Establishment Clause analysis is whether the challenged practice has longstanding historical or traditional roots — e.g., ***Marsh v. Chambers,*** 463 U.S. 783 (1983) (upholding legislative chaplain in part because the tradition may be traced back all the way to the first federal Congress); ***Van Orden v. Perry***, 545 U.S. 677 (2005) (narrowly upholding a Ten Commandments display on the statehouse grounds in Austin, Texas, which had existed for 40 years without inspiring any complaint, where evidence of an impermissible governmental purpose was lacking).

5. **A Closer Look at the Leading Cases in Each of the Three Establishment Clause Scenarios**

a. Category #1: Government **Aid** to Religious Institutions (Whether in the Form of a Subsidy or Service)

1) ***Walz v. Tax Commission,*** 397 U.S. 664 (1970) (upholding property tax exemptions for churches) shows that fiscal support for religion through the tax system will not be regarded by courts as governmental imposition of religion upon nonbelievers.

2) ***Mueller v. Allen,*** 463 U.S. 388 (1983) (upholding a state tax deduction for expenses incurred for "tuition, textbooks, and transportation" for elementary and secondary schoolchildren, regardless of whether they attended public or nonpublic schools).

a) Focusing on Rehnquist's majority opinion, note what he says about "the private choices of individual parents."

b) Rehnquist stresses that any aid flowing to parochial schools from this tax deduction stems from the PRIVATE DECISIONS OF PARENTS to send their kids to religious, rather than public, schools.

c) Thus, he says, any aid to parochial schools under this law is attributable to **private**, not to governmental, decision making.

d) Accordingly, "no 'imprimatur of State approval' can be deemed to have been conferred on any particular religion, or on religion generally."

e) This "private choice" theme later looms large in ***Witters***, ***Zobrest,*** and ***Zelman***.

3) In ***Witters v. Washington Department of Services for the Blind,*** 474 U.S. 481 (1986), the theme of "private choice" surfaces again as the Court rejects a challenge to a statute that authorized the payment of public funds to blind persons for vocational rehabilitation services where the recipient planned to use the funds to pay tuition at a Christian college.

    a) The key to the Court's "private choice" analysis was the fact that any payment under the program went "directly to the student, who transmits it to the educational institution of his or her choice."

    b) Thus, "any aid provided under [the] program that ultimately flows to religious institutions does so only as a result of the genuinely independent and private choices of aid recipients."

4) ***Zobrest v. Catalina Foothills School District,*** 509 U.S. 1 (1993) (rejecting a challenge to a program in which the government funded sign-language interpreters for deaf children — regardless of whether they attended public or parochial schools).

    a) The key for Rehnquist, writing for the Court, is again the "private choice" theme — the daily presence of a government-paid interpreter inside a Roman Catholic high school stems here from the **private choice** of the boy's PARENTS, not from any STATE decisionmaking.

5) ***Agostini v. Felton,*** 521 U.S. 203 (1997) (in a 5-4 opinion, with Justice O'Connor writing for the majority, the Court held that a federal program that funds remedial instruction and counseling of disadvantaged children in public and private schools does not violate the Establishment Clause, even though it results in public employees being sent to teach inside parochial schools).

    a) This decision overruled ***Aguilar v. Felton,*** 473 U.S. 402 (1985), which prohibited public school teachers from conducting such classes on the premises of parochial schools.

6) ***Mitchell v. Helms,*** 530 U.S. 793 (2000) (continuing a trend toward relaxing the restrictions on government aid to religious schools, the Court here rejected an Establishment Clause challenge to a federal program that places computers in the classrooms of public and parochial schools alike).

    a) In upholding this legislation, the Court overruled still more of its Establishment Clause precedents — this time repudiating:

        1. ***Meek v. Pittenger,*** 421 U.S. 349 (1975) (striking down a statute that authorized the lending of instructional materials, such as maps and laboratory equipment, to nonpublic schools, and the furnishing of public

school employees to provide such services as remedial reading instruction and counseling at nonpublic schools); and

2. ***Wolman v. Walter,*** 433 U.S. 229 (1977) (striking down a statute that authorized the lending of instructional equipment to students in nonpublic schools and the payment of costs incurred by nonpublic schools on field trips for secular courses).

7) ***Zelman v. Simmons-Harris***, 536 U.S. 639 (2002) (rejecting an Establishment Clause challenge to a "school choice" voucher program that funneled tax dollars to low-income families for tuition aid in sending their children to private schools, even though 96% of the participating students used the money to enroll in religious schools).

a) Here in ***Zelman***, the "private choice" theme (earlier developed in ***Mueller***, ***Witters***, and ***Zobrest***) comes to full fruition, serving as the centerpiece of the Court's rationale.

b) ***Zelman*** makes clear that the "private choice" theme applies specifically to application of the **effect prong** in funding cases — and that the presence of true private choice will **prevent** a violation of the effect prong, even if the challenged government funding goes to a disproportionately high percentage of religious recipients.

Essay Advice

For states that also test Constitutional Law in essay form

If you get an Establishment Clause issue involving **aid** to religious schools, be sure to discuss the "private choice" theme, which has played an increasingly prominent role in recent years. If the ultimate target of the aid is school children, and the aid is given to secular and sectarian schools alike, the Court will uphold the aid program so long as the aid finds its way to religious schools due to the "private choice" of parents to send their children to those schools.

Zelman shows that across-the-board aid will be upheld even if religious schools receive a disproportionate share of it, so long as the disparity is attributable to private choice.

b. Category #2: Government **Identification** with Religion (Often Featuring Religious **Symbols** Erected on, in, or Near a Government Building)

1) ***Lynch v. Donnelly,*** 465 U.S. 668 (1984) (rejecting an Establishment Clause challenge to a municipal Christmas display that featured a crèche surrounded by a large number of secular elements, including a Santa Claus house, reindeer, candy-striped poles, and a sign that read "Season's Greetings").

    a) Justice O'Connor's concurring opinion here is regarded now as significant and influential for broaching the "no endorsement" test and for reformulating ***Lemon*** IN TERMS OF endorsement.

2) ***County of Allegheny v. ACLU,*** 492 U.S. 573 (1989) (holding unconstitutional a freestanding nativity scene on the main staircase of a county courthouse, but upholding the display of a Jewish menorah placed next to the city's Christmas tree and a statement declaring the city's "salute to liberty").

    a) In ***Allegheny***, a majority of Justices adopted O'Connor's "no endorsement" analysis as a general guide in Establishment Clause cases.

3) ***Capitol Square Review & Advisory Board v. Pinette,*** 515 U.S. 753 (1995) (refusing to treat as an Establishment Clause violation the unattended display of a privately-owned cross — among other religious symbols — on government property).

    a) Note what Justice O'Connor says in her concurrence: "When the reasonable observer would view a government practice as endorsing religion, [it] is our **duty** to hold the practice invalid."

c. Category #3: Religious **Teachings** or **Practices** Within a Governmental Ceremony or Institution

1) ***Stone v. Graham,*** 449 U.S. 39 (1980) (striking down a Kentucky statute requiring that a copy of the Ten Commandments be posted on the walls of each public classroom).

2) ***Engel v. Vitale,*** 370 U.S. 421 (1962) (striking down a public school policy recommending that classes recite aloud an official prayer, drafted by the New York Board of Regents, professing belief in and "dependence" upon "Almighty God") (writing for the Court, Justice Black asserted that "in this country it is no part of the business of government to compose official prayers for any group of the American people to recite as a part of a religious program carried on by government").

3) ***Abington School District v. Schempp,*** 374 U.S. 203 (1963) (striking down a state law requiring that ten verses from the Bible be read aloud at the opening of each public school day).

4) ***Wallace v. Jaffree,*** 472 U.S. 38 (1985) (striking down an Alabama statute authorizing schools to set aside one minute at the start of each school day "for meditation or voluntary prayer") (the bill's sponsor stated that it was "an 'effort to return voluntary prayer' to the public schools").

5) ***Edwards v. Aguillard,*** 482 U.S. 578 (1987) (striking down a Louisiana statute requiring public schools to teach "creation science" whenever they taught the theory of evolution) (the Court found that "[t]he preeminent purpose of the Louisiana legislature was clearly to advance the religious viewpoint that a supernatural being created humankind").

6) ***Lee v. Weisman,*** 505 U.S. 577 (1992) (striking down a policy that authorized prayer at public school graduation ceremonies).

    a) Justice Kennedy, writing for the Court, announced the "anti-coercion" principle as a baseline standard for Establishment Clause violations.

    b) Key facts: the school's principal exerted editorial control over the **content** of the prayer, and, given the context of a graduation ceremony, "subtle coercive pressures" existed here that effectively compelled students to attend and to participate in the prayer.

    c) That the prescribed prayer here was NON-sectarian does not make it, when uttered at the State's **behest**, any less a violation of the Establishment Clause, Kennedy asserts.

    d) This is because the Religion Clauses "mean that religious beliefs and religious expression are too precious to be either proscribed or prescribed by the State. The design of the Constitution is that preservation and transmission of religious beliefs and worship is a responsibility and a choice committed to the private sphere.... [T]he central meaning of the Religion Clauses...is that all creeds must be tolerated and none favored."

    e) State-sponsored religious exercises send a message to the citizenry that the State disavows its duty to protect **each** person, **each** faith, from a State-created orthodoxy.

7) ***Santa Fe Independent School District v. Doe,*** 530 U.S. 290 (2000) (striking down a public high school policy permitting student-led, student-initiated prayers prior to football games).

C. THE FREE EXERCISE CLAUSE

1. **Recommended Analysis**

    a. In assessing a Free Exercise claim, inquire which of the following two scenarios best describes your facts:

> ***Free Exercise claims — 2 scenarios:***
>
> ***Scenario 1:*** Purposeful interference by the government with a religious belief or practice.
> *Governing standard:* strict scrutiny.
> *Likely outcome:* The Free Exercise claim will probably succeed.
>
> ***Scenario 2:*** A generally applicable law, not specifically directed at religious practices, that nevertheless impinges upon their exercise.
> *Governing standard:* rational basis review.
> *Likely outcome:* The Free Exercise claim will probably fail.

2. Examples of Scenario #1: Purposeful Interference by the Government with a Religious Belief or Practice

    a. ***Church of the Lukumi Babalu Aye v. City of Hialeah,*** 508 U.S. 520 (1993) (striking down city's newly-enacted ban on "ritual slaughter" as applied to animal sacrifices conducted by the plaintiff church as part of its practice of the Santeria religion — where the legislative history of the ordinance revealed that, far from being neutral, its central purpose was to ban the Santeria worship service from being conducted anywhere within the city).

    b. ***Torcaso v. Watkins,*** 367 U.S. 488 (1961) (striking down a provision in the Maryland Constitution that required state officials to declare their belief in the existence of God).

3. Examples of Scenario #2: A Generally Applicable Law, Not Specifically Directed at Religious Practices, that Nevertheless Impinges Upon Their Exercise

    a. ***Reynolds v. United States,*** 98 U.S. 145 (1879) (upholding a Mormon's conviction for bigamy).

    b. ***Braunfeld v. Brown,*** 366 U.S. 599 (1961) (rejecting a Free Exercise challenge by Orthodox Jews to a Sunday closing law). The ***Braunfeld*** Court observed: "[To] strike down [legislation] which imposes only an indirect burden on the exercise of religion [would] radically restrict the operating latitude of the legislature. [We] are a cosmopolitan nation made up of people of almost every conceivable religious preference. [Consequently,] it cannot be expected, much less required, that legislators enact no law regulating conduct that may in some way result in an economic disadvantage to some religious sects and not to others because of the special practices of the various religions."

c. ***Sherbert v. Verner,*** 374 U.S. 398 (1963) (writing for the Court, Justice Brennan opinion distinguishes ***Braunfeld*** and holds that unemployment compensation cannot be **denied** to a woman fired by her employer for refusing to work on her church's sabbath, Saturday).

d. ***Wisconsin v. Yoder,*** 406 U.S. 205 (1972) (holding that, as applied to the Amish, Wisconsin's compulsory school attendance law violated the Free Exercise Clause in compelling the Amish against their religious beliefs to send their children to school beyond the eighth grade).

  1) In arriving at this result, the Court announced a Free Exercise balancing test considerably protective of individual liberty.

  2) Writing for the Court, Chief Justice Burger acknowledged the state's "interest in universal education," but insisted that it be balanced "when it impinges on fundamental rights and interests" to assure that "there is a state interest of sufficient magnitude to override the [Free Exercise] interest."

  3) "[Only] those interests of the highest order and those not otherwise served," he wrote, "can overbalance legitimate claims of free exercise of religion."

e. In the wake of ***Sherbert*** and ***Yoder***, then, the Court's Free Exercise analysis inquired whether the challenged law substantially burdened a religious practice and, if so, whether the burden was justified by a compelling state interest.

f. But the Court refused to apply that balancing test in the most significant Free Exercise case of recent years: ***Employment Division v. Smith,*** 494 U.S. 872 (1990).

  1) In ***Smith*** (per Justice Scalia), the Court rejected the Free Exercise claim of a Native American who was denied unemployment benefits after being fired from his job for partaking in the sacramental use of peyote — part of a religious ritual in the Native American Church.

  2) "The right of free exercise," wrote Scalia, "does not relieve an individual of the obligation to comply with a 'valid and neutral law of general applicability'" on the ground that the law compels conduct his religion forbids or forbids conduct that his religion compels. **Such laws are valid if they are rationally related to any legitimate state interest.**

g. ***Smith*** did not overrule ***Sherbert*** and ***Yoder***, but it certainly crippled them — effectively boxing them into their facts.

h. In the wake of ***Smith***, then, we are left with the two scenarios identified above: rational basis review for Scenario #2, with strict scrutiny reserved only for those unusual situations (e.g., ***Hialeah***) where government intentionally burdens religious belief or practice (Scenario #1).

4. Bear in mind, finally, that Free Exercise claims are greatly weakened if advanced by the denizens of certain "restricted environments" — soldiers and prisoners.

a. **The Military** — e.g., ***Goldman v. Weinberger,*** 475 U.S. 503 (1986) (employing an extremely deferential standard in rejecting a Free Exercise claim by a Jewish officer in the Air Force who was barred by regulations from wearing a yarmulke indoors).

b. **Prisons** — e.g., ***O'Lone v. Estate of Shabazz,*** 482 U.S. 342 (1987) (applying a "reasonableness" test for Free Exercise claims brought by prison inmates) (prison officials, citing security concerns, barred Muslim inmates from traveling within the prison to attend a weekly congregational service mandated by the Koran).

D. THE "NO MAN'S LAND" BETWEEN THE ESTABLISHMENT AND FREE EXERCISE CLAUSES: AFFIRMATIVE MEASURES BY GOVERNMENT TO ACCOMMODATE RELIGION

1. Affirmative steps by government to promote or accommodate the free exercise of religion may cross the line into an Establishment Clause violation.

2. The test for judging whether an accommodation is permissible or whether it runs afoul of the Establishment Clause: Is the government alleviating a regulatory burden for religious exercise or is it conferring a special benefit upon religion?

3. The former will likely survive judicial scrutiny, but the latter may be deemed violative of the Establishment Clause.

4. **The Leading Cases:**

a. ***Corporation of Presiding Bishop of the Church of Jesus Christ of Latter-Day Saints v. Amos,*** 483 U.S. 327 (1987):

1) Upholding the religious organizations exemption in Title VII, which permits such organizations to engage in employment discrimination on the basis of religion.

2) This was an unsuccessful challenge by a janitor who lost Mormon employment due to his failure to abide by the prescribed abstinence from tobacco, coffee, and alcohol.

b. ***Texas Monthly v. Bullock,*** 489 U.S. 1 (1989): In a 5-4 decision authored by Justice Brennan, the Court strikes down a statute that exempted religious publications from a state sales tax.

1) Brennan: By directly targeting for government aid those publications that **promulgate** the teachings of religious faiths, this Act conveys an unmistakable message of endorsement that violates the Establishment Clause.

2) Scalia's dissent: The tax exemption here is a permissible accommodation of religion; this should be an easy case because **taxing** religious publications might well violate the Free Exercise Clause.

c. ***Board of Education of Kiryas Joel Village School District v. Grumet,*** 512 U.S. 687 (1994): Striking down as an impermissible accommodation of religion the creation of a special **public school district** for a village that served as a religious enclave for a sect of Orthodox Jews.

1) Writing for the Court, Justice Souter focused on how the State of New York had singled out this religious sect for special favorable treatment, thus violating the Establishment Clause principle requiring government neutrality among religions.

2) Kennedy's concurrence focused on the fact that New York created the school district by drawing political boundaries **on the basis** of religion.

3) Scalia's dissent: How can New York's helping this tiny minority sect effect an ESTABLISHMENT of the Satmar Hasidim?

d. ***Larkin v. Grendel's Den,*** 459 U.S. 116 (1982): Striking down delegation of veto power to churches over the issuance of liquor licenses to nearby restaurants.

5. At the end of the day, the standard by which to reconcile these religious accommodation cases is to inquire: Is the government alleviating a regulatory burden for religious exercise or is it conferring a special benefit upon religion?

6. Only the **former** instances will be deemed consistent with the Religion Clauses.

VI. THE SECOND AMENDMENT

A. The Second Amendment provides: "A well regulated Militia, being necessary to the security of a free State, the right of the people to keep and bear Arms, shall not be infringed."

B. Though ratified in 1791, the Second Amendment did not receive any significant attention from the Supreme Court until 148 years later, in ***United States v. Miller***, 307 U.S. 174 (1939), where the Court upheld a federal firearms statute in the face of a Second Amendment challenge. The ***Miller*** Court construed the Second Amendment narrowly, holding that it protects the right to keep and bear arms for certain military purposes, but that it does not bar the government from regulating the non-military use and ownership of such weapons.

C. Almost 70 years later, the Court reexamined the Second Amendment and adopted a dramatically different view. In ***District of Columbia v. Heller***, 128 S. Ct. 2783 (2008), in a 5-to-4 ruling, the Court held that Second Amendment gun rights are not confined to military uses or service in a militia — instead, **the Second Amendment confers an individual right to own a gun for private use**.

D. Justice Scalia's majority opinion in ***Heller*** struck down a handgun ban in the District of Columbia. Though he did not overrule ***Miller***, straining instead to distinguish it, ***Miller*** can only be regarded now as a dead letter.

E. Though ***Heller*** leaves many unanswered questions, it is clear now that any outright ban on handgun possession in the home will violate the Second Amendment. The ***Heller*** Court also held that the Second Amendment is violated by requirements that lawfully-owned firearms must be kept at home in a disassembled or inoperable state, because such a restriction effectively thwarts the capacity for immediate self-defense.

F. ***Heller*** leaves plenty of room for continued gun regulation. Justice Scalia specifically states that "nothing in our opinion should be taken to cast doubt on longstanding prohibitions on the possession of firearms by felons and the mentally ill, or laws forbidding the carrying of firearms in sensitive places such as schools and government buildings, or laws imposing conditions and qualifications on the commercial sale of arms." 128 S. Ct. at 2816-17. Justice Scalia describes the foregoing restrictions as "presumptively lawful" under the Second Amendment, and he adds that the list is illustrative, not exhaustive. *Id.* at 2817 n.26.

G. An individual's Second Amendment right to own a gun for private use operates as a restriction not only upon the federal government but also upon state and local governments by way of the Fourteenth Amendment. ***McDonald v. City of Chicago***, 130 S. Ct. 3020 (2010)

Printed in Dunstable, United Kingdom

91218905R00087